MACK HANAN

Profits

W·I·T·H·O·U·T

Products

MACK HANAN

Profits

W·I·T·H·O·U·T

Products

How to Transform Your Product Business Into a Service

American Management Association

New York • Atlanta • Boston • Chicago • Kansas City • San Francisco • Washington, D.C.
Brussels • Toronto • Mexico City

7-20-11

This book is available at a special
discount when ordered in bulk quantities.
For information, contact Special Sales Department,
AMACOM, a division of American Management Association,
135 West 50th Street, New York, NY 10020.

This publication is designed to provide accurate and authoritative information in regard to the subject matter covered. It is sold with the understanding that the publisher is not engaged in rendering legal, accounting, or other professional service. If legal advice or other expert assistance is required, the services of a competent professional person should be sought.

Library of Congress Cataloging-in-Publication Data

Hanan, Mack.
    Profits without products : how to transform your product business
into a service / Mack Hanan.
        p.   cm.
    Includes index.
    ISBN 0-8144-5132-2
    1. Service industries—United States—Management.   2. Customer
service—United States—Management.   I. Title.
    HD9981.5.H36   1992
    658.8'12—dc20   92-27376
                                                                          CIP

Consultative Selling℠ is a registered trademark of Mack Hanan.

Printing number

10 9 8 7 6 5 4 3 2 1

To **Tim Noonan,**
　Who saw the need
To change the way
　His company did business
Because he could see
　Where they must go
While others could see only
　Where they had been

Contents

Preface: The Great American Self-Deception

In the early 1980s, Japan's Ministry of Trade and Industry (MITI) commissioned a then little-known junior strategist, Nabuo Arakawa, to head up a top-secret mission, puckishly code-named Operation Level Playing Field.

With a handful of acolytes and a pocketful of yen, Arakawa set about to tilt the international balance of trade in favor of Japan. His method was ingenious. Through his agency's wide-flung contacts all over the world, Arakawa inserted into the American political-economic dialogue the concept of a Malcolm Baldrige National Quality Award in such a way that American politicians and business managers came to think of it as their own.

Once the award was announced and product quality had thereby become an irrevocable policy directive for the American economy, Arakawa watched with a sense of fulfilment as the scenario he had set in motion worked itself out exactly as he had planned it—or, as he was fond of saying with characteristic modesty, exactly as if he had planned it himself.

Beset by a generation of anxiety about the "fit and finish" of American products and fired up by a neo-Freudian quality envy, American manufacturers began a feeding frenzy to "win the Baldrige." En masse, they focused their collective corporate energy inward, just where Arakawa had hoped they would, on their research and development quality, their engineering quality, their manufacturing quality—on what eventually became known as TQM (total quality management) and was humanized by people sitting around kneecap to kneecap in endless quality circles during what would otherwise have been business hours.

Virtually all looking outward toward where the markets were and what margins could be gained by adding value to them came to a full stop with the introduction of the Baldrige in 1987.

Total quality meant exactly what it said. Arakawa had seen to it that quality would be uncompromising at the 99.9997 level of perfection that engineers call Six Sigma. This permitted only a rate of 3.4 defects per million parts or transactions, which for practical purposes came to be regarded as near-zero defects. In order to achieve defectless perfection, immense resources of time and money and concentration of the most expert people would have to be forced all the way up the cost-benefits curve, where attempts to attain the final 20 percent of perfection can cost up to 80 percent or more of a product's total investment. This unremitting quest would tie up each company's best and brightest development people for unfathomable man-days on each project, causing them to miss cycle after cycle of emergent new opportunities while doggedly perfecting obsolescent ones.

"We serve no wine," these manufacturers took pride in saying symbolically, "before its time." But time, as it tends to do increasingly in modern business, came and went in an ever-faster rhythm.

The market, meanwhile, got short shrift. As a sop, "customer satisfaction" was tacked on to the tail end of the Baldrige list of the several components of quality. But in the Baldrige context, it meant satisfaction with a supplier's product quality and the quality of product-related services far more than the quality of customer growth that a supplier should be helping to generate or the quality of a customer's competitiveness that the supplier should be helping to increase.

Nobuo Arakawa knew when he began his strategy what American business managers would only find out later. Through his reverse engineering of the results of ten years worth of installing TQM in Japanese companies, Arakawa had discovered that getting down to a 10 percent defect rate was about the best you could hope for. Even at that, it could take ten years to bring defects down that far. At the outset of the Baldrige, Japan already had a decade-long head start to TQM, and Japanese managers were rapidly losing their enthusiasm for it. It was simple for Arakawa to convince them that it was safe to export.

It was Arakawa's plan to let American managers invest the next ten years in understanding that when they finally got to a 10 percent defect rate on each batch of 400 units, they would still be left with forty customers who would have a 100 percent defective experience with their products. While these recurrent dissidents were being satisfied by expensive forms of amelioration such as product recalls and replacements, any remaining profits that had survived Six Sigma would be soaked up. Meanwhile, Arakawa, as a profit-centered sideline, would flood the United States with T-shirts and bumper stickers that said "Quality is Free."

Under Arakawa's scheme, America's preoccupation with Baldrige quality would give Japan a ten-year period of grace to take over its next earmarked portfolio of markets. As the decade neared its end, Arakawa's long-range plan was to migrate American managers from TQM to ZDM (zero defects management), where truly zero defects might be manageable with just a little bit more concentration on products and a little bit more blindness to markets. Taken together, these two strategies would give Japan a full generation of economic security as well as, not quite incidentally, guaranteeing Nobuo Arakawa's personal golden parachute into early retirement.

As the Arakawa strategy took over American business, products became the focal point of every manufacturer's costs, but not of the margins that could recover them. In a short time, quality became equality and once-competitive products became noncompetitive commodities whose sole remaining differentiation was their discount rate.

Instead of achieving the holy grail of "sustainable competitive advantage" (a classic oxymoron, since an advantage that could be sustainable would be monopolistic and not competitive; if it were competitive it could not be sustainable), American manufacturers would be stuck with unsustainably noncompetitive and cost-disadvantaged products at equal levels of higher quality. As a result, margins would be few and far between. The quality advantage would still be in the East while Western margins steadily headed south.

American companies are still busy trying to score the magic number of 750 Baldrige points to qualify for a National Quality Award. Little do most of them know that many of their Japanese competitors would have scored well over 1,000 points way back in the 1980s. But quality above the market's level of "good-enoughness" earns no margins. From the 1990s on, margins are no longer to be found in quality, but only in the commensurate value it can yield its customers.

Once Nobuo Arakawa hit on the concept of adding more competitive value to customers as the source of margins instead of adding more quality to products, inventing the Baldrige as the Great American Self-Deception came easy to him. He does not bother to deny it any longer. His prescience has made him popular as a favored doubles partner of the tennis-playing elder Japanese kieretsu to whom he loses deferentially three afternoons each week. These ritualistic matches mean little to him. He is secure in his secret knowledge: The Baldrige, no matter how many winners it has, has won more for him than it ever will for them.

Suffused by the Japanese equivalent of glasnost, Arakawa is periodically motivated to tell it like it was. From time to time, he finds himself doodling in a manuscript that may become a behind-the-scenes confession called "The Parted Kimono." But while Arakawa doodles, our margins burn: Margins are disappearing from the world's products; products are disappearing from the world's manufacturers; and manufacturers are disappearing from the world's economy— all because we focus on products in and of themselves instead of as components of services that more directly touch the profitmaking power of our customers and, for that reason, can command margin power in return. Arakawa may write the book on how business has changed. *Profits Without Products* is the book on how to change the way we do business as a result.

MACK HANAN

Profits

W·I·T·H·O·U·T

Products

1

The Flight of Margins From Products

What happens when you reach the point that Frito-Lay did in 1991 when "it was not possible to sell potato chips any cheaper"—when all the traditional remedies, such as making your operations more efficient, reducing the capital costs associated with your manufacturing, or putting pressure on your suppliers to sell to you at lower and lower prices, have been tried and failed?

When happens when you are IBM or Apple Computer, hated rivals, and in the same year of 1991 come to the same realization that neither of you will ever make major profits again selling desktop computers—when the product lines of both of your companies have already been cut back to eliminate the dogs, your markets have been reduced, and your people have been let go by the tens of thousands so that an alliance to join forces is the only way left for either of you to stay in the personal computing business?

In similar fashion in industry after industry, and in company after company within them, margins have fled their products. They have fled from computer boxes, where they have fallen from 15 percent in 1981 to 9 percent in 1991; they have fallen from beer barrels, oil drums, cornflakes crates, and from yards of textiles, tons of steel, and gallons of gasoline. Yet margins are what businesses are all about. Aside from being the only thing that you can take to the bank, margins prove the value that your business adds to its customers. They attest to the expertise that you have put into developing and manufacturing your products and the applications and implementation expertise that will ensure that these values are fully brought out in your customers' operations. A high-margin business is a high-value-adding business. Its margins are its proof of value. Without them, there is no way for a business to invest to add still more value in the future.

Why have margins fled their products? They have become squeezed between manufacturer-driven quality standards that have made almost all competitive products good enough and market-driven standards of performance that have ruled out any meaningful differentiation between them. A company's discount performance (*not* its proprietary product performance) has become the industry-wide differentiator. In some businesses it has become so bad that it is cause for dancing in the aisles when discounts can be held to 48 percent instead of 52 percent.

In a global economy where today's breakthrough is tomorrow's knockoff, where quality has become universally equalized, where competitive product features and benefits are distinctions without a difference, and where proprietary differentiation would only add to a customer's costs of refitting and retraining, selling has become selling on price. In turn, selling on price has become selling off price.

No matter where you do business, just about every market is overstocked with virtually equal products. Most of them cancel each other out quickly. The survivors fight for share of mind, share of shelf, share of sales time, and share of market. Even for the winners, their life cycles tend to be so short that their researchers and developers have little time and fewer profits to get their next cycle of technology up and running. If they come up dry and miss a cycle, they may be out of the race for several years or forever. In many technology-intensive industries, products live by the same code as the Mafia: "Live fast, die young, and have a good-looking corpse."

Desperately Seeking Margins

With margins no longer to be found "in the box," it is becoming increasingly difficult for hardware-type businesses to make money or to get funding with investment money. Will Poduska is a "box man" who has run two high-technology companies, once blowing $200 million in venture capital. Poduska has this to say about his experience in trying to run a third product-based business: "It is becoming extremely difficult, if not impossible, for a small entrepreneurial company to effectively compete as a supplier of computer hardware systems" if its competitiveness is going to be box-to-box.

It is also becoming extremely difficult, if not impossible, for product-based businesses to acquire $200 million in venture capital. Japanese investors in American high-technology businesses are learning to avoid hardware manufacturers. According to Shoichi Fujikawa, president of Jafco, Japan's leading venture capital firm, "There is no money to be made in hardware."

Back in the 1980s, one of the most debatable issues was between owning your own capabilities or partnering to get access to their use without having to own the underlying assets. A common debate would be framed like this: Do we need to own computer technology as an internal resource or do we just need to be able to sell in the computer marketplace? The question of the day in the 1990s is no longer focused on technology. It now concerns products: Do we need to make products to be a player in the computer marketplace or do we need to provide a service in which our products and those of other manufacturers are modules?

Every company's room for maneuver around its hardware has been getting smaller. If you try to entice one more year's worth of mileage out of the traditional product-based business model, you will be in trouble. You will replicate the experience of Aluminum Company of America's (ALCOA) CEO Paul O'Neill, who refused to believe that margins had fled from his sheet aluminum business and tried to maintain what he called "leadership pricing." It cost him $100 million in lost sales.

Campbell Soup Company's Convenience Foods Division learned the same lesson when it tried to use promotions and cents-off coupons to move its frozen foods. Marketing expenses rose 6.4 times faster than sales, bringing down pretax margins to about half the industry average. No matter how much Campbell spent, there was no way they could "make it up on volume." Once the expenditures stopped, volume went back to its starting point.

Along with aluminum and packaged goods retailing, other industries have been transformed into services far more rapidly than the companies that compose them. Steelmaking became a service industry in the early 1980s. Steel service centers began to contribute more to steel company profits than melting and smelting. The added value from doing business with a steel company shifted from the quality and availability of molded alloys to the quality of its consultative advice in selecting and applying the steels that each customer required.

The computer industry also became a service in the 1980s. The value of doing business with a computer manufacturer migrated from its hardware to its ability to customize the most cost-effective implementation and integration of total information systems. Yet the companies that made up the industry went right on selling boxes on their performance features and benefits—the very things that their customers were signaling had lost their power to command the high margins that offer proof of high value.

When differentiation vanishes, margins go with it. Pit bull price wars simply move market shares around. Microsoft Corporation and Lotus Development Corporation go after each other like pit bulls. In their 1991 war, Microsoft offered deep-dish discounts to Lotus users who would trade in their 1-2-3 spreadsheets for Microsoft's Excel. Microsoft lost money on the deal and the Lotus share of spreadsheet sales was driven down to less than half the market. It was only a matter of time before Lotus retaliated by offering 1-2-3 to Excel customers for less than $150 compared to a list price of $595. This time it was Lotus that lost money. Its stock price also fell $1.50.

Insight into what has become an almost universal problem can be gained from the computer industry's history since the mid-1980s. Earlier in the decade, a time now known as the industry's "good old days," product life cycles could run from three to five years. This allowed time to recoup research and development investments and still earn twice the margins on sales of average industrial companies. But by the 1990s, computer manufacturers were averaging returns that were 20 percent or more lower than other manufacturers while their average profit margins had dropped almost by half. At Digital Equipment Corporation (DEC), it was being said that "We have to sell 70 percent more unit volume every year just to stay even in revenue," to say nothing about profits.

Gone forever was the typical 1980s scenario that saw the $300,000 sale of a midrange computer bring a 65 percent gross margin. If a sales representative sold only four minicomputer systems a year, his or her company would make a gross profit of $700,000. In the early 1990s, customers could buy equivalent computing performance for only $150,000. The manufacturer was able to take home just a 40 percent gross margin. In order to bring in the $780,000 gross profit of the 1980s, thirteen minicomputer systems would have to be sold.

If you go with the flow of margin flight, you can make money if you frankly acknowledge that your hardware is a commodity. Sun Microsystems Inc. outsources almost all of its parts. It keeps employee headcount and infrastructure to a minimum. At only a 7 percent profit margin, it has managed to earn an 18 percent return on equity. By contrast, IBM had still been trying to make money from hardware. In 1990, when IBM finally saw the light, it described the resulting restructuring of its sales, marketing, and support staffs into services as the biggest movement of people since the troops came home at the end of World War II.

Back when adequate returns on hardware were still the rule rather than the exception, IBM was one of many companies that were able to extract a consistent premium "qua IBM"—just by being who they were. But as Bank of America has said about IBM, "Their 30 and 40 percent premiums don't wash here anymore [since] we've not been successful in quantifying the added value of working with IBM."

As profit margins have been shrinking in electronics, metals, industrial and farm equipment, motor vehicles, petrochemicals, telecommunications, and scientific equipment, managers have been asking: Where can I add value to stop the bleeding?

The answer is hardly ever in the product and increasingly in service. If you are in electronics and you want to add value to a car manufacturer, it will most likely come from your applications knowledge of automobile electronics systems rather than from the systems themselves. If you are a chemicals processor, added value will come from helping your customers save money and make money by applying your specialty chemicals rather than from the chemicals themselves. Nalco Chemical Company calls its specialty chemicals "high margin products." But their margins really come from Nalco's "Strike Forces" that help customers prevent equipment corrosion in their manufacturing processes by proper use of the chemicals.

Aside from the rare and extremely costly breakthrough products that are ultrachancy, unpredictable, and can still be cut off at the pass by knockoffs, money in the 1990s will only be made in service. Transforming your product-based business into a high-margin service will be the single most crucial strategy that will make you rich. In one industry after another, one company is making this discovery before its competitors:

• Cooper Tire & Rubber Company is the industry standard supplier for independent tire dealers. Throughout the 1980s, Cooper compounded its annual profits at an average rate of 22 percent by consulting with its customers on how they could maximize their own profits reselling its products in the automotive aftermarket.

• In the paper industry, P. H. Glatfelter Company averaged a return on equity of 20.3 percent in the early 1990s by "servicing the hell" out of its customers as consultants in lowering their costs and expanding their revenues. Glatfelter's megacorp competitor, International Paper Company, is twenty times its size and has been returning only 6.5 percent on equity.

• A. G. Edwards, the brokerage business correlate of Glatfelter, is a $500 million company with profit margins four times greater than Merrill Lynch, a $12 billion competitor. Edwards spends most of its time "figuring out how to provide better services" as consultants to its customers.

• Metaphor Computer Systems took a consultative approach to selling the same applications software program that multibillion-dollar competitor IBM sold as a product. Metaphor made its product into a revenue generator for clients; IBM was perceived as a cost to its customers. Metaphor counseled on improving user profits while IBM appeared to disadvantage them. Metaphor got its margins. IBM ended up buying Metaphor.

• Philip Morris is becoming a service business for its supermarket customers in order to ensure access to their outlets for its consumer packaged products. Its services include in-store stocking, merchandising and promotions, evergreen inventory management to avoid stockouts, and market research and marketing planning for store chains and even individual stores.

• Kennametal Inc., a metalworking and mining tools manufacturer, has gone into the distribution services business. Playing twin roles as manager of inventory facilities and integrator of tool storage systems, Kennametal acts as sole provider of its customers' tool needs, including products made by competitors.

In the words of Arden Haynes, chairman of Canada's Imperial Oil, all these companies can say the same thing: "If our organization structure was the right model for yesterday, it is certainly not the right one for today."

Giving Service a Name

Doing business as a service opens you up to many different kinds of flexible money-making practices that are beyond the scope of product-based companies and far beyond their margin capabilities. In a service mode, you can act as a purchasing agent for your clients. Moving upscale, you can hold yourself out as their prime contractor on major projects. Or, at the other end of their supply chain, you can be a distributor for their products and services along with your own. You can be their business advisor or technical consultant. You can be their co-investor in joint ventures or a manager of some of their key operations. None of these options is dependent on your products. Yet your products can play a role in many of them.

If you have a product-based business, you make and sell "a better mousetrap." When you transform your business to a service, you may still make mousetraps but you will sell them without selling them. Instead, you will sell the value of your customers' reduced costs from goods no longer subject to damage by mice and the expanded revenues that will accrue from having more undamaged goods to sell. You will base your price on the sum total of the value you add to your clients, not on the cost of your mousetraps. Your mousetraps will bear no price at all.

To give your service a name, it can be called "zero mouse management," a subfunction of customer inventory control. Under the terms and conditions of the way your business works, you may mouseproof your customers' warehouses, integrate the optimal mix of mousetraps, cheese and mouse disposal services, and manage their application as an out-sourcer. Your service would be customized for each company's inventory function that you managed. You would be paid a professional fee based on the annualized value of each customer's cost savings and revenue increases.

Your fee would be proportional to each customer's added value so that it represents a win-win rate of return for both of you. The ratio of customer costs to acquire your service to customer benefits as a result of using it would be the major purchase decision required to put you in business. Your fee would pay for the expertise of your mouse managers and the mousetraps and cheese and related services necessary to implement each customer's annual profit-improvement plan.

You could continue to manufacture your own mousetraps or outsource them in the same way you would obtain the cheese. As long as they were good enough to help you achieve your customers' objectives from zero mouse management, you would never have to tender proposals for them, publish spec sheets on them, or debate their competitive merits.

Tomorrow's "better mousetrap" will be a service. It will be founded on three basic principles:

1. *If you make a product, do not sell it.* Instead, sell the service to which your product makes a contribution. Digital Equipment Corporation is picking up on this by freeing its customers from the requirement to make any product purchases at all. Instead, Digital will "rent a result" by assuming ownership of a total solution system that includes hardware, software, services, and training. The customer pays Digital a professional fee based on results.
2. *If you sell a product, you do not have to make it.* Instead, buy rather than make.
3. *If you make and sell products as part of your service, do not push them.* Instead, push your customers closer to an improved competitive advantage.

The penalties for violating these guidelines are unforgiving. Even an alliance will fail to remain an alliance if you enter into it in a solely product-based mode. Baxter International found that out in the middle of its six-year $250-million-a-year sole supplier contract with Hospital Corporation of America. Hospital Corp. has been one of Baxter's largest customers and closest business allies. Nevertheless, Hospital Corp. gave its 130 hospitals the authority to sidestep the long-term, sole-source supply and distribution contract and seek other bidders than Baxter who could offer better prices. Baxter was forced to respond by offering $10 million in price concessions, the very downside that its alliance was designed to avoid. While privately grumbling about the flight of loyalty, Baxter said in public only that "there are ups and downs in any long-standing customer relationship."

Failing With Product-Based Remedies

The long-term universal decline in product margins is here to stay. Its global nature has caused a generalized profits recession. After-tax earnings from continuing operations—the money that you can take to the bank—have been dropping almost everywhere. In industries where profits rather than cash flow have been the accustomed catalyst for growth, there is no longer any dependable way to jump-start a business. In other industries, the traditional strategy of raising earnings by raising prices has been nullified. Cutthroat competition forbids it. Parity products give it no justification.

In product-dominated companies, more earnings are currently coming from cost-cutting write-offs, spin-offs, and layoffs than from margins. Price wars are continuous. Every time a price is lowered to increase a product's share of market, profits are eaten into. The push to keep gaining market share in order to be a low-cost producer is guaranteed to keep prices low.

As profit margins fall, managers can no longer afford to support overhead in the form of technical staffs, sales engineers, and even salespeople. They are leaving their lowest-end products unsupported by the very factors that have given them value. All that they can do then to control their margins is to continue to cut costs and prevail on their vendors to cut their own margins. To stay alive in such a mutual poverty network, everybody loses. The definition of a "good business" becomes one with few fixed assets.

The odyssey of Cincinnati Milacron shows what typically happens when a product-based business gets into margin trouble and turns to alternate product-based remedies instead of biting the bullet to transform its business from products to service.

When Japanese competition penetrated Milacron's machine tool markets with higher quality tools at lower prices, margins fled Milacron's products and it still could not match Japanese prices. Milacron tried to find new margins through diversifications into higher technology products such as robots, lasers, and semiconductor wafers. Even though Milacron could price higher in its new markets, the costs of rapid new product development and the investment in long cycle times of educational selling that were required proved to be even higher. After several marginless years, Milacron decided to "go back to basics" in its traditional machine tool business.

By the time it got there, the cupboard was bare. Foreign-made machine tools owned half the U.S. market. Their manufacturers, most of them based in Japan, were well along in making many of their products right on Milacron's home grounds.

Milacron's return to its knitting, to standard tools such as lathes and other machines that cut and form metal parts, represents its last stand. It is also one of the last stands for the American tool industry that Milacron pioneered. By reducing its manufacturing costs as much as 40 percent, Milacron can go head to head with the Japanese on price in about one-fifth of its machine tool lines. The margins on the other four-fifths of its products will determine Milacron's ability to absorb the multimillion-dollar costs of its modernized plants and the opportunity costs of forfeiting the futuristic assets that could have resourced the Milacron of the year 2000 and beyond.

The question has been raised if Milacron can out-Japanese the Japanese. But the real issue is whether Milacron can out-Milacron itself. Will it continue as a manufacturer of machine tools or can it transform itself to serve its customers' higher margin needs to manage their profit contributions from metalworking?

Can Milacron hold its machine tools in one hand behind its back and hold out its other hand to customers as "experts in solving your kind of metalworking problem"? Can it say, "You have the opportunity to expand the value currently being contributed by your metalworking operations"? Can it say, "We are the industry standard of cost-effectiveness in metalworking. Here are the values we are normally able to add to your type of operations. How much more advantaged would you be if we can help you approach the values we are normally able to add?" Or will Milacron go on selling machine tools?

Staying too long as a product-based business, no matter

how high margined it may be to start with, is a failure-ridden strategy. It is the story of Compaq Computer Corporation, more than any other company the symbol of successful product manufacturers of the 1980s. Starting out in 1982 with a product drawn on the back of a placemat at the House of Pies restaurant in Houston, Texas, Compaq became a billion-dollar business in just four years. Yet in just four more years, the bottom fell out. Compaq reported its first quarterly loss when its high performance technology was exceeded by low-end clones whose costs were half of Compaq's. As a result, the clones could undercut Compaq's prices by as much as 50 percent.

Without differentiation, Compaq found itself a costly high-quality manufacturer without commensurate margins. As soon as it discounted, its perceived image of exclusive branded quality disappeared. Compaq had become just another clone. From king of the hill, Compaq became the deposed emperor who had no margins. In 1992, ten years after its founding, Compaq had learned one of the most important lessons for the 1990s. It would no longer go after peak performance at all costs. "Now we're asking what the customer's requirements are."

Every product in the 1990s is just one degree of separation from clonehood. *Clone* is today's buzzword for commodity, since it meets the commodity definition of things equal to the same thing being equal to each other. The "same thing" in many cases is a market's open standards that all suppliers are required to meet. Open standards rule out the proprietary performance benefits that have traditionally justified high margins. Once standards become open, differentiation based on exclusivity is legislated out of a market by its customers' fiat. They no longer want to pay its costs. Nor do they want to become locked into perpetual dependence on its supplier.

Open standards save customers on purchasing costs. But they go far beyond. Standard products enable customers to set one-time standard performance guidelines to manage them and standard programs to train managers and operators in how to supply them. They also allow customers to standardize their purchasing processes, becoming vendor-independent. As a result, sellers and their products have become interchangeable parts. So have customer employees who can operate any product once they have learned how to operate any other product. No one needs to be reeducated, ending retraining expenses and the attendant costs of disruption. In a single stroke, open standards allow a customer to be product-independent, supplier-independent, and employee-independent.

Managing the Business of Customers

Whenever products are sold as products, slide valves are slide valves, health and beauty aids are health and beauty aids, and a dollar is a dollar when offered on loan by a bank.

The same is true for *services*. Services do not make a service business. Only by making your customer businesses more competitive can you become a service business. You can do this with products *or* services. But migrating from a line of products to a product line composed of services will not afford you any added margin power if you sell the services like products, or if the services are equally undifferentiated. Services sold at their hourly "manufactured" cost are commodities. Services that are replicas of competitive services are also commodities. Neither will improve your own profits or help you improve the profits of your customers.

There are just as many "me-too" commodity service opportunities as there are commodity products. This is true even of professional services. Unless a service can be differentiated by the profit impact made by its provider, it will be bought and sold on price. Look-alike services merit look-alike prices, pegged at the lowest common denominator.

When Xomox positions itself as a service business that provides the managers of its customers' chemical processes with an improved contribution to corporate profits, its slide valves become differentiated. They are able to command margins that no competitor comes close to equaling. When Johnson & Johnson positions itself as a service business that provides its supermarket customers with an improved profit contribution from health and beauty aid sales, its products become differentiated. They are able to command margins that no competitor comes close to equaling. And when Citibank positions itself as a service business that provides its borrowers with consultation on improving the yields on their loans, its dollars become differentiated. They are able to command margins that no competitor comes close to equaling.

Not one of these products has undergone change. None differs significantly from the others. In the case of Citibank's dollars, there is obviously no difference at all. What has changed is the way these businesses have positioned themselves. Instead of going to market as product-based businesses that price their products and give away their services, they have transformed themselves into service businesses that price the value their products and services add to their customers' competitive advantage. Their products bear no price tags of their own. They would act as toe tags to their margins if they did.

Businesses that are transforming themselves to services from being product-based are discovering that they can add more value to customers—and receive more margin in return—if they serve them rather than supply them. Serving means applying, implementing, installing, and measuring the value they add to their customers, consulting on how to maximize its contribution to customer cost structures or cash flows, educating customer people in the most cost-effective way to achieve the contribution they have counseled, and even managing customer operations with them or for them.

In competition with providers of services like these, either in conjunction with their own products or someone else's, no product supplier can come close to their values. Consequently, no product supplier can come close to their margins.

Xomox is in the service business of managing chemical process improvement. It deals in minimizing its customers' process downtime and maximizing throughput. Johnson & Johnson is in the service business of managing the health and beauty aid category for its supermarket customers. It deals in minimizing their costs of stockouts and maximizing their revenues from increased turnover. Citibank is in the business of managing its customers' yield on borrowed funds. It deals in maximizing their rates of return and minimizing their turnaround cycle between borrowing, payback, and borrowing more. Each company has given up on trying to increase its customers' *perceived value* of their products. They appeal instead to each customer's *received value* as a result of the value-adding service they provide.

Customers need all the management help they can get. Other than for the few industries where technology breakthroughs are patentable to the point where competitors are legally deterred for long periods of time and for the even fewer companies in these industries that can count on developing breakthrough products on a more or less consistent basis, the margin power of products—the ability of a product to command more than its market would prefer to bear—has become a nostalgic relic. Between 1980 and 1990, profit margins in many worldwide bellwether industries fell as much as 50 percent. Price lists degenerated into wish lists and more business ended up being bought by discounts than being sold on margins.

Exploring Service Business Models

It is not only clones that have lost their margins. Even never-before and one-of-a-kind new products have become margin-endangered species. Maturity has always made product values gray in the dark. But all kinds of products are being regularly discounted even on introduction. The margins they used to take for granted just for being new and the period of grace from competition that went along with newness are long gone. Yet today's new products take increasingly longer to develop, cost more, and have ever shorter commercial life cycles within which to replenish the investment in their development.

Even in long-established product categories, the same cycle of predictable events takes place over and over again.

Earnings fall on stagnant or sometimes rising revenues, selling costs skyrocket, and layoffs and downsizings contribute to a pervasive business malaise. Newton's laws have become applicable to product-based businesses: Profits at rest tend to remain at rest; margins in downward motion tend to remain in downward motion.

None of these events are new. All of them have been occurring under the noses of many top managers. Some have slept through it; others have hoped against hope that what turned out to be a step change in their businesses was only going to be a temporary blip on their growth curves after all.

Hewlett-Packard Company is by no means alone, but that does not make it any less typical of how leadership at the top has been acting as followership of the past. In the mid-1980s, when it was becoming evident that HP's vaunted engineering and manufacturing excellence would no longer by itself be able to justify undiscounted margins, management circulated memos instead of a redirection of capital that could have transformed its business. The memos asked for middle managers' opinions on whether computers were becoming mature at a time when the number of annual units being shipped was still growing but their dollar value was increasing at an ever lower rate—a better answer than any manager's opinion. But it was easier to exchange opinions than to face facts.

A half dozen years later, in 1991, long time CEO John Young said about HP's "surplussing" thousands of its people and downsizing many of its businesses, "If I had my life to live over again, I would have done it earlier, maybe as much as two years."

The "it" that John Young eventually did was to gut HP. In an industry where product performance had been expanding almost fourfold every three years throughout the early 1980s while price was falling in inverse relation to computer processing speed from 10 to 20 percent, the death knell for product margins should have been loud and clear. The need for a service orientation was past due. Yet HP was still bogged down in searching for a customer orientation for its products.

A better model can be found in John Young's own industry in the IBM of the 1960s and 1970s, before Big Blue forgot what its customers had spent almost twenty years teaching it: The essence of profit is rarely product based—it is customer based; the essential service is never product related—it is customer related.

When Tom Watson, Jr., ran IBM, he made it a service business. "We make computers," he said. "But we sell the improved profits that our computers can make for our customers." Even though IBM's computers were most of the time "unburdened by technical superiority," it had become a cliché to say that "Nobody ever got fired for buying IBM." Other computer manufacturers were showing customers better speeds and feeds and superior bits, bytes, and bauds. IBM, in contrast, was showing them a better contribution to their profits from computer technology. IBM showed $15 million in new sales to Black & Decker by solving out-of-stock problems in its highest margin power tools. IBM showed Church's Fried Chicken how it could earn an additional $25,000 in first-year sales from each new store it opened by ensuring its optimal location. Neither customer saw fit to be shown competitive computers or to discount IBM's margins.

By the mid-1980s, IBM had lost its way. Growth had stagnated because of a sales mix composed of more than 70 percent products. IBM's entire multibillion-dollar business had become organized around its product groups. It would take until 1995, according to Chairman John Akers, before 50 percent of IBM's revenues would come again from service. In the interim, 1990's "Year of the Customer" was going to have to become every year.

IBM is getting its feet wet in true service businesses by leading from its strengths. It has taken its expertise in storing and transmitting computerized data and multimedia mixing of text, video, and sound into a joint venture with Time Warner, Inc. The venture will integrate information, education, and entertainment services and manage their nationwide distribution. Time Warner is contributing its program inventory and showbusiness experience. Toshiba, the third partner in the venture, gets stuck with manufacturing the electronic control boxes that sit on top of the system's TV monitors.

Putting Relationships Before Products

Product suppliers and service providers come at their businesses 180 degrees apart. If you are product-based, you sell products and give away product-related services. As a service provider, you furnish a Kaizen-type continuous improvement of the customer operations that you can affect, and service-related products are merely modules of your total system.

You ask different questions. As a supplier, you are preoccupied with asking, "How can we make a better product?" Service providers ask how they can help their customers make better profits:

- What increases in productivity can we help a customer achieve in his operations that we sell to?
- What increases in customer margins can we contribute to his products that we affect?
- How can we improve a customer's current ratio between his initial costs and his life-cycle costs of ownership in dealing with us?
- How can we help a customer to achieve a better balance between his short-term cash flows and his longer-term profits from our work together?

When you transform a product-based business into a service, you learn how to touch your customers at the points where your products and product-related services are applied rather than where they are purchased. At your customer's points of application, which is where his users are and not his buyers, you will be able to get your arms around your customer's priorities while they are still hot off the press in the form of his business plans. But the only way you will be able to access them is by moving up the value chain from one end to the other: going from the supplier end where your products, your plants, and their processes form your asset base all the way up to the provider end where your assets are concentrated in the ability of your people to grow their customers—*to be of service to their customers' competitive advantage.* When you can touch your actual end-user customers in this way, you will be able to manage your margins. Even more, you will be able to manage your customer relationships at the apex of account control.

For this reason, service providers are called relationship managers, profit consultants, and business advisors to the managers of their customers' business operations. Because their relationship is essentially fiduciary, being focused on improving the profitability of customer competitiveness, the customer managers they relate to are called clients. The standard of performance for each consultant with each client is the continuous improvement of the client's return on doing business with the consultant.

Modeling Service Opportunities

When you become a service business, client profits become the products you sell regardless of the products you make. Client profit improvement becomes the nature of your service. Products are still important contributors to your clients' improved profits. But they play a correlary role along with your project management skills, your product application and implementation technologies, and your customer information and education capabilities. Your fees will be based on the total value you add to each client's operations. Because you sell the value, your value-based fees will ensure high margins. You will not sell your products nor will you price them. You will sell them by *not* selling them.

If you want to claim or reclaim margin power in the 1990s, your sole recourse will be to rethink the basis of your business. Margin opportunity over the foreseeable future is clearly going in the direction of managing improvements in the organization, work flows, and cash flows of a client's critical success functions, processes, and operations. The "best of breed" practices of the 1990s will be founded on improvements in client competitiveness that stimulate client business growth. This is the mission of a service provider, not a product supplier.

Client processes, not your own processes, will have to become your business arena. Your margins will be in direct proportion to how much you can improve their contributions to profits. Products will disappear from your sales force's bags. Application skills that can put products to work and consultation and education skills that can empower your clients' workers will take their place. They will be dependent on how much you know about each client's operations and how you can affect them—in other words, on your abilities to help manage a client's business rather than only the ability you have to manage your own.

The new types of client relationship managers who will be required to sell the values of continuous improvement will be money managers with acute process smarts in the client business operations where they can make their impact. Their clients will be business managers of cost centers and profit-centered lines of business. Your money managers will work with three basic service models:

1. Integrating a client's functional systems to improve their cost-effectiveness
2. Reengineering a client's operating processes to rationalize or restructure them
3. Managing or co-managing a client's facilities as an insourcer or outsourcer

If you make one or more of these service models your own, you will have the only upside potential for your margins that the 1990s will give you. If you choose to remain a product-based business, your margin potential will be all on the downside. The customers you can continue to sell to directly will continue to squeeze your margins. The systems integrators, process engineers, and facility managers who control their client accounts will increasingly intervene between you and your customers. You may never touch your customers directly again. Your sales will be integrated by their integrators. Your terms will be the integrators' terms. Your prices will be their prices. Your margins will be what you can preserve, not what you deserve.

Each of these models carries with it its own caveat:

- Integrate your clients' systems or risk being disintegrated out of them or integrated into a competitive supplier's integration.
- Reengineer your clients' operations or be engineered out of them by a competitor who does.
- Manage your clients' facilities or business categories or become a product supplier to a competitive manager.

The good old days of product supremacy were good, but they are old. In the mid-1960s, the United States was manufacturer to the world and made money at it. America processed more goods than the next nine industrial nations combined. One company alone, General Motors, made more profits each year than the ten largest corporations in all of Western Europe. By the 1980s, everything had changed in the ways that goods could be produced and services delivered by traditional industries. New, small companies in upstart industries found that they were no longer bound by the barriers to entry that had made success unlikely in historic businesses. They borrowed their entry fees and niched or outflanked entrenched competitors. The combination of new technologies and new ways of doing business proved fatal to product scarcity or uniqueness. As soon as automated productivity and equal quality could be found almost everywhere, and almost everywhere at the same high levels, margins based on differentiation became a thing of the past.

Every manager's challenge in the 1990s is to run, not walk, away from doing business as usual and start getting comfortable with doing "business as unusual." General Motors chairman Robert Stempel put it this way in 1992: "The biggest challenge is to get this company to be where we have to be in the year 2000. We are obviously going to have to do things differently than we have for eighty years." One of those things is to define your business as a service. Another is to define the nature of the service as helping customers manage their businesses better. This will turn out to be the only way you will be able to manage your margins.

As a consequence, *business transformation* has become one of the 1990s' buzzwords. It covers a multitude of changes, all of which it attempts to encompass in an unending process of restructuring: multiple skillsets for everybody so that no one is indispensable, new methodologies to get more work done in shorter times with fewer people, and an acceptance of cultural diversity to soften the traditional "my way or the highway" monolithic corporate cultures of the 1980s. But none of these changes will add up to a hill of beans unless a business can make more money after it transforms itself than before. The only way that any business is going to be able to do that is to gain the margin advantages that only service businesses can command.

2

How to Manage the Segue Into Service

One company after another is taking its businesses apart and putting them back together with new technologies, less inventory, and reduced turnaround time from entering an order to delivering it. The objective of all this restructuring and reengineering is to maintain current production levels in substantially smaller manufacturing space with fewer workers. In these ways, managers hope to slash billions in annual costs and boost productivity. But when it comes time to sell the new and revamped products that come out of these reconstructed businesses, how will they make their margins in competition with identical products manufactured under identically reorganized conditions?

The proliferation of low-cost nonproprietary products that has come out of the restructuring of American industry has made margin attrition inevitable. Applications, not products, are today's principal source of margins because they are the principal source of value. If you have a dollar to invest in the growth of your business, and you choose to put it into products instead of service, you will be taking the very real chance of allocating more and more of your money for less and less margin. If you end up with application, information, education, and consultation skills that are anything less than world class, you will be carrying on your business in a marginless cul-de-sac of your industry. The only way out is to commit to service, which will enable you to go with the flow of value and, along with it, margins.

The transformation process from being product-based to a service provider can be modeled along lines like these:

1. A petrochemicals processor sells a product called *Stim* to oil companies. The product stimulates producing wells to maintain their yield on a constant basis. As a new product, it is exclusive. It needs to be used only once a year. Competitive products must be used at least three times a year. Each time a well is stimulated, it goes on downtime. Sales revenues are lost. Labor and chemical costs are incurred. Because Stim reduces these costs and helps maintain cash flows, it commands a premium price.

2. Stim is replicated by competitors. It becomes a commodity. Its premium margins disappear. Its sales costs rise. As its price falls, manufacturing costs must be continually reduced in order to maintain margins. Stim's manufacturer figures that there is one supplier too many in the market. If one would quit, the others could make money. But each waits for one of the others. The stimulation business lacks stimulation.

3. Stim buys business by giving away free applications and measurement and information services with each product sale. These free services erode Stim's margins even further. Competitors replicate the same services. If each supplier could charge for its services, they could be profitable. But no supplier wants to be first, fearing loss of its product business to the others.

4. Stim's manufacturer "goes out of business" as a product supplier, repositioning its business as a service. The nature of the service is the management of predictable productivity. Management is provided under a facility management contract. The contract assesses a professional fee that bundles applications, measurement, information, and consultation services with "all the Stim your wells can drink." None of the components in the bundle bears a price. The fee is based on the added value to each customer of being able to

predict marketable yields together with the amount of re-duced maintenance and downtime costs. Each management agreement carries a kicker: If production exceeds the base level contracted for in the agreement, the market value of the incremental sales will be shared by the facility manager and his customer.

If you substitute *fertilizer* for *oil well stimulator*, a chemicals processor who serves agbusinesses can follow the same scenario. He can transform a product-based business to a service that helps manage yield for large-scale farmers and farm cooperatives. By a similar substitution, the scenario will work equally well for manufacturers of industrial products, providers of health care and financial products, and produc-ers of every other kind and description.

Segueing into a service business from a product base is a matter of mindset, capabilities, and customer data.

Your mindset must undergo a change from being fixated on what "we do" and "our products and our competitors" to focus on how your customers can do better as a result of working with you to make continuous improvements in their products, services, and systems. Your business purpose must be to help them become advantaged against their own com-petitors, not concern them with yours. You must be able to relocate the shrine of your capability base from your engineer-ing and manufacturing resources to your peoples' skills in installing your products, applying them, training customer people in their most cost-effective use, and consulting on maximizing their value. These areas of expertise will be your most precious resources. With them, you will be able to partner with your customers' people and grow your busi-nesses together.

Since service businesses live or die based on their peo-ples' hands-on application skills, your databases must be replete with the customer problems and opportunities that compose the leads for applying your skills. You will have to know the critical success factors that make your customers competitive, how to reduce the costs and increase the reve-nues that they contribute, and how to set up and manage a continuous stream of profit-improvement projects to make each customer more advantaged.

The signal difference between a business that sells a service while giving away related products and a business that sells products while giving away related services is shown in Figure 2-1. In Model A, the added value contributed by the service—not the service itself—is the star. Because it defines the business, it becomes the "product." As such, it bears the price tag. The product and service components of the system that are necessary to provide its value are unpriced because they are never sold, only supplied.

In Model B, the product is the star that defines the business. Product-related services are bundled into a product-based system. The product bears most or all of the system's price. Most of the product's related services, if not all, are free. They exist to support the product's price. The value derived from the system's installation and implementation is generally unknown; in any event, it has no bearing on price.

Suppliers of product-based systems go to market prepared to cost-justify their price. One way or another, they will sacrifice margins to make a sale. Either they will give away more service free or more free services or they will discount their asking price. By contrast, service providers go to market prepared to cost-benefit their value. They will prove the amount and timing of the incremental cash flows they propose and play what-if games to test alternate scenarios of profit improvement: What if we add to or subtract from the investment? What if we substitute a lease for purchase? What if we advance payback by ninety days by dividing the investment into two installments?

Instead of justifying their price as an added cost, service providers search for the single best return on the customer's investment that will maximize their added value. Their investment will act as the price. It will be proportional to its return. Unlike the product vendor and his customer, the service provider and his client have the same objective: Each wants to maximize the client's return. Since the investment will vary directly with it, everyone must win.

Figure 2-1. Customer-value/product models.

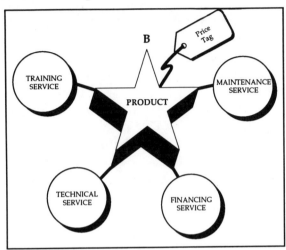

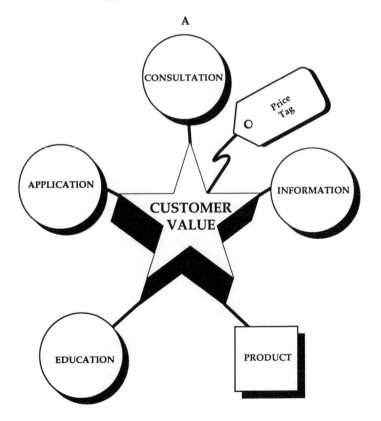

Suppliers who sell from the product model sell *product performance* benefits in return for a disproportionately small price. Service providers sell the value added to *client performance* in return for a proportionate investment. That is why providers are able to be accepted as business partners, whereas vendors are not. It is also why providers get their margins.

When Tom Watson, Jr., was chairman of IBM, he told people who envied IBM's earnings that "If you don't have my philosophy, you won't have my margins." His philosophy was based on the service model. His margins were generated by it.

Delighting the Customer

Many chief executives are making it the order of the day for their people to "delight the customer"—to keep customers happy and make them "feel good about you." They apparently see no discrepancy between this customer-oriented sense of mission and the product-based objectives they set for their businesses: objectives such as "a 24 percent increase in units shipped and installed" and "a 12 percent decrease in operating expenses." Their objectives would be more in keeping with their mission if they were also customer oriented on a parallel track so they could be expressed in customer-specific terms such as "Managing our customer's assets to help him achieve an increase of 24 percent in units shipped for his line-of-business A and a decrease of 12 percent in its operating expenses." In this way, customer delight would be the natural outcome of business mission.

There is no way that a business based on products can achieve delightful outcomes for its customers. Only a service that helps a customer improve the management of his assets can do the job. Product-based chief executives have a difficult time understanding this. They fail to distinguish *servicing* their customers in the manner of the Maytag Man from *serving* their customers' needs to grow. They cling to the belief that the value their businesses create is in their products and that services are simply supportive add-ons to product sales. For this reason, when left to their own choices, product-based businesses are amateurs at transforming themselves into services.

In the health care industry, Becton-Dickinson's hypodermic needles are a case in point. In order to support their margins, BD has been giving away free training programs to improve nurse productivity, reduce hospital costs of wasted needles, and cut down on patient problems resulting from their improper use that raise insurance rates and litigation costs. For years, the training programs have been regarded as an added cost of sale for the needles—a sweetener of needle sales—rather than as a value in themselves that could drive needle sales instead of help prop up their sagging margins. If they were priced in proportion to their value, even if it were to represent a mere one percent improvement in each hospital customer's current costs, thousands of times more earnings would accrue to BD than from sales of hypodermic needles. Under these circumstances, the hypodermic needles could be given away free.

This type of role reversal between products and service is difficult for product-based business managers to contemplate. Product thinking tends to dominate their definition of service. When Hewlett-Packard's computer sales and margins began to go in opposite directions, the company created a single division out of its consulting services, customer training, and systems integration capabilities and called it Professional Services. But HP's definition of service was totally technical, having nothing to do with the management of customer business strategies that predetermine the needs, configurations, and values of integrated information systems. HP's definition of consultation was equally technical: how to implement a system.

Professional Services was simply a flank strategy to sell more computers. Its work was limited to customer operations "where there is a lot of HP product content" and where there presumably could be more. Service was still being used as a strategy to support products rather than customers.

Putting Your Finger on Where You Are

The transition of a business from being product-based to a service is a continuum. Figure 2-2 will show you where your own business is on the continuum. If you are in the early stages represented by points 1.2, 1.3, and 1.4, you are behind the margin curve. You are giving away service value to make up for declining product value. Only when you get to point 2 will you be in position to get ahead of the curve.

A product-only business will be quickly pulled into becoming a product-plus-services business by customer demand. Product-related services such as technical support, training, and financing become necessary to help customers purchase your products and make sure they get their full value from them. As supports to product sales, the services will be given away free.

As products mature into commodities, they come under increasing price pressure as the penalty for losing their differentiation. They then tend to be bundled into product and service systems in which the price of each system will most likely be determined by its product components. The services

Figure 2-2. Product-to-service cycle.

---

1. Product Business

    1.1. Product

    1.2. Product-related services

    1.3. Bundled systems of products and product-related services

    1.4. Stand-alone services

2. Service Business

    2.1. Service-related products

    2.2. Services only—no products

---

will remain unpriced. Either they will be presumed to have no value on their own or their value will be unknown. In either event, their suppliers will be reluctant to charge for them since they have taught their customers that they do not have to pay to obtain them.

At point 1.4 in Figure 2-2, a demand will be perceived for the customization of some services on a stand-alone basis. Training, information, and consultation are usually the first services to find a market of their own. But due to its heritage, a product-based business will sell services as if they were products. It will price them on a cost-plus basis, calculated on the hourly rate of their providers. They will no longer be free. But their prices will still have no relation to their value.

As a result, it will be only a short while before services become subject to the same margin pressure as products. Someone will always be able to replicate them and provide them cheaper.

When a business transforms into a service at point 2, it may add service-related products to its stand-alone services and bundle them into systems. In this case, the price of a system will be based on the value it adds to the customer operation in which it is installed. The service component of the system will bear no price. Neither will its related products. Both will be "free." Only their combined value will be charged for.

In order to maintain a competitive advantage, the service may need to add a more comprehensive value than the products of its supplier can contribute by themselves. Or the products of other suppliers may be more cost-effective in contributing to the system's value. This will open up the system provider to buy products he does not make so that he can sell the most cost-effective integrated system.

The final step in the evolution from being product-based to a service comes at point 2.2 with the realization that it is not necessary to manufacture any products in order to sell them as components of an integrated system. A business can then become a services-only provider, either as a systems integrator for its customers—a kind of general contractor—or a process reengineer whose business is the restructuring of customer operations for which it may or may not choose to supply products.

A third option is to act as a facility or category manager for customers, either insourcing the management of a customer operation or outsourcing it as an independent asset manager.

Margin opportunity increases progressively throughout the evolution from point 1.1 through point 2.2. With or without products, service businesses make their money from managing or comanaging their customers' business functions, prescribing optimal systems of product and service solutions and supervising their application, installation, and implementation. Whatever the specific nature of their service may be, they are essentially management services whose value is determined by the competitive advantage they add to their customers. This is the basing point for their price, which is expressed as a management fee.

If you are behind the margin curve anywhere in point 1 of Figure 2-2, you are incurring unaffordable opportunity cost from suboptimized margins. Every day is costing you. Until you can put your finger on point 2 in the figure, a competitor who can will be eating your lunch.

Acquiring a Service Mindset

As long as your business prices your products, sells your products, and is organized around product groups, you will go to market every day with a product mindset. A service mindset requires you to rethink a wholly different concept of your business: how you think about what you do, for whom you do it, and why.

A service business provides accelerated growth to its clients. It serves their growth objectives by helping them seize currently undercapitalized opportunities to become more competitive. It also develops new opportunities with them that can be capitalized at a high rate of earnings. The value of a service business to its clients is calculated by the sum total of new capital it helps them generate and the rate at which it helps them generate it.

Expertise, not products, is the core competency of a service business. But neither the expertise nor the products of a service business are priced or sold. The "product" of a service business that is priced is the value it adds to its clients. Its price, which is called a professional fee, is based on its value.

The clients of a service business pay for their growth, not its components in the forms of products and product-related services. In effect, they buy one-dollar-plus for every one dollar they invest. Since a service business customizes its value for each client it serves—as well as for each project it works on for each client—all of the values it delivers will be different. None of its "products" will be standardized.

The general statement of mission for a service business is not to be the best manufacturer or largest market shareholder but to make its clients better manufacturers and larger market shareholders. Service businesses have client dedication built into them. They judge how good they are by how much better they make their clients. Their clients base their "customer satisfaction" with them the same way.

When you ask a service business manager, "What do you make?" the answer should be, "We make our clients more competitively advantaged—we make our clients richer."

The objectives that a service business sets for itself are the results of the growth objectives it sets for its clients. A service business grows as a derivative of its clients' growth, not at their expense. For every dollar of client growth that a service business provides, it may set a fee of twenty cents, for example, for the first one hundred dollars and participate on a sliding scale for its contributions thereafter.

If a service business cannot grow a client as much as one of its competitors, or as quickly or as reliably, it may lose the client to the competitor. With direct client access foreclosed, the losing service business may then have to serve the competitor by acting as a subcontractor of expertise or products to him. This will reduce the losing service business to acting as a second-tier provider to its competitors. Its expertise and products will be sold on their hourly rates and performance ratings, after which its competitors will integrate them into client operating systems or manage their contribution to a client's facility. The wheel will have turned full circle back to low-margin or no-margin sales. The lesson is that losing service businesses devolve into product businesses that end up as sources of supply to winning service businesses.

A service business has a one-to-one relationship with its clients just as if it were a line or staff extension of their businesses and responsive to the same objectives. They become Siamese twins who are joined at the objectives.

The mission of a service business to become the best by making each of its clients *their best* is accomplished in two ways:

1. Maximizing the profit contributions made by a client's current operations that it can affect, either by helping the client invest his assets more cost-effectively or enabling the client to divest some of them.
2. Adding to the value of future operations by helping a client to minimize development or acquisition costs, maximizing their cost-effective application, and continually improving their profit contribution throughout their life cycles.

Struggling to Get Out

Inside every product business is a service business struggling to get out. The latent service business within one of your current product businesses shows up quickly when you plan it "backwards." Start with your customers' businesses as your products and product-related services currently relate to them. Ask yourself questions like these:

- Where do our products go when we sell them? What are the customer business functions, operations, or processes in which our products are installed, applied, and used?

- What do our customers do in these business functions that we may be able to help them do better, do differently, or do more cost-effectively, either cheaper or more productively? Where are the main cost clusters that use labor or materials or energy most intensively? Where are the main crunch points for scrap production, downtime, or maintenance? What are the main issues for critical decisions? Where are the markets whose sales opportunity remains unrealized?
- What other business functions are networked with the ones where our products go? What related processes or operations are dependent on a reliable, uninterrupted, and cost-effective work flow?
- What standards of performance are the managers of these business functions being held to? How is their performance measured in terms of cost control, revenue generation, productivity expressed as cycle times, meantimes, and downtimes, and customer satisfaction?

When you guide your thought process to go with the flow of your products into the operating processes of your customers, you will be taking the first step in transforming your business to a service.

The second step involves another close-order drill composed of two questions:

1. If customers are using our products to facilitate their internal operating processes, can we help them to use them more cost-effectively by reengineering their processes to reduce their costs or increase productivity? Can we help them integrate our products with the products of other suppliers? Can we help them to manage the resulting integrated systems better or can we manage them better as their outsourcers?

2. If customers are using our products to facilitate their sales, can we help them sell more or sell more cost-effectively or at higher margins?

Figure 2-3. The value chain.

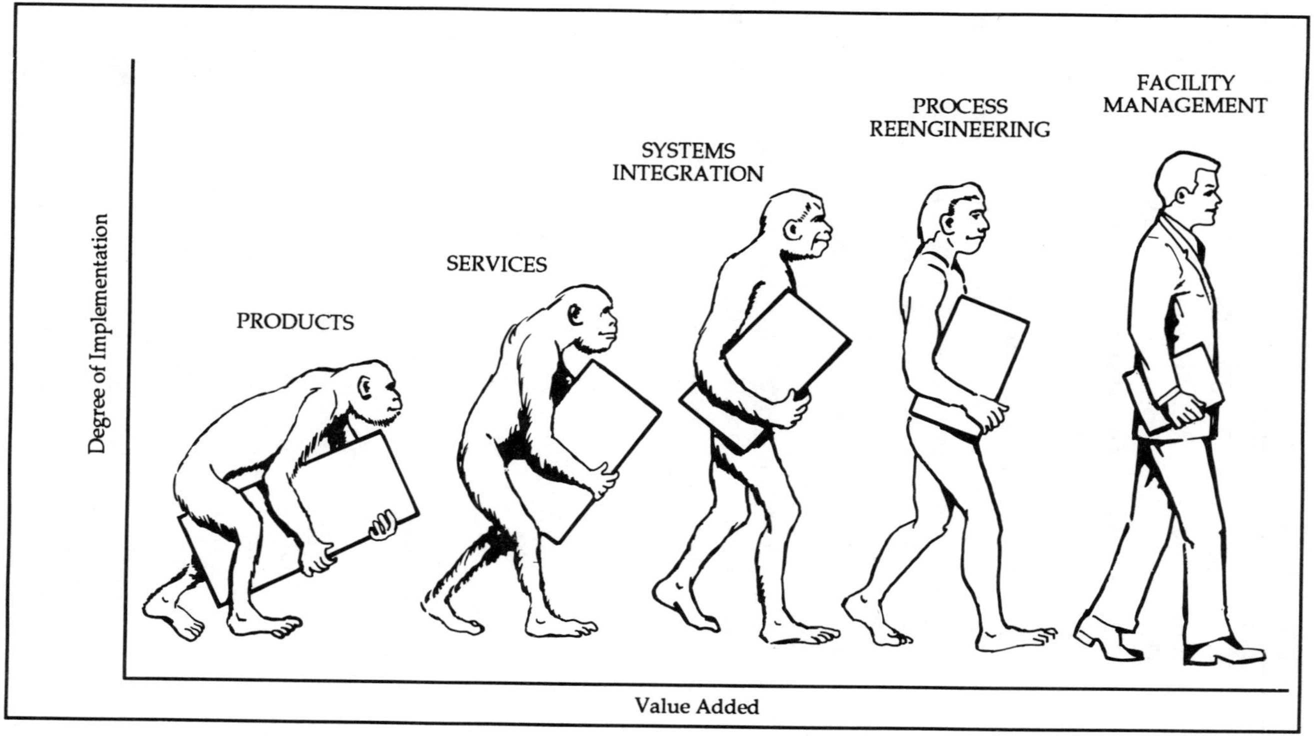

PRODUCTS

SERVICES

SYSTEMS INTEGRATION

PROCESS REENGINEERING

FACILITY MANAGEMENT

Value Added

Degree of Implementation

The third step asks you to set up three scenarios for a service business to use as straw men:

1. "We can integrate a customer function's equipment into a more optimal mix that makes an improved contribution to profits." This scenario can lead you to provide a systems integration service.
2. "We can reorganize, restructure, or reengineer the way the customer's function currently works." This scenario can lead you to provide a process reengineering service.
3. "We can manage a customer's function more cost-effectively, either in-house or as an outsourcer." This scenario can lead you to provide a facility management or category management service.

The rank order of these three scenarios composes a value chain. Each scenario is progressively less product-based and progressively more of a management and comanagement service. As Figure 2-3 shows, the higher up the value chain your scenario takes you, the greater value you provide and the greater margins you can command.

You can add high-margin value as a systems integrator who takes a customer's current process and makes it function better. You can add more high-margin value if you restructure the process. You can add the most value if you manage a client's function with him or without him. As a manager—either your client's managing partner or his partner in management—you can integrate its current system, reengineer it, and operate it. The closer you come to doing what your client has been doing for himself, the greater your value will be in freeing up his resources, permitting him to reallocate them, and running them more cost-effectively.

The three service scenarios reveal the essential characteristics of all service businesses: They improve a customer's current configuration of a function's assets, reallocate them, or manage the function.

1. Services that *improve a client's installed asset base* can help him revitalize a process with a customized turn-

key system composed of the optimal mix of assets or integrate the component assets of an ongoing process more cost-effectively.

2. Services that *reallocate a client's assets* can help him optimize their use by rearranging a process or restructuring the way it flows.
3. Services that *take over the management of a client's assets* can help him downsize his asset base by divesting a cost center or reducing the cost contributions of its management, labor, and materials. They can also convert a cost center into a profit center by renting out its excess capacity after they have reengineered it.

Since more value derives from the applications of technology than from the products that contain its raw power, there is a continuous flow of commodity pressure up the value chain shown in Figure 2-3. Nothing along the chain that can be homogenized will be safe from margin erosion. Since all the applications on the value chain touch customer operations more intimately than products—because they consist of human contacts rather than electronic or mechanical or chemical ones—they are considered to be downstream from the products to which they add value.

The value flow of the 1990s is moving inexorably downstream. The red tide of commodity pressure pursues it. Both are headed toward the source of margins.

Manufacturing companies that fail to come up with downstream values on which to put a price may find it difficult to go on manufacturing. From the moment when service took over as the sweet spot of profitability, manufacturing has been relegated to a reward. Making products upstream is the beneficiary of making profits downstream. In companies where this is true, manufacturing has become the result of value creation rather than the major cause.

If you want to go on being a manufacturer, transforming your business into a service will earn you the right to do so by earning the margins that will fund you. Your products will derive their birthright from the earnings that come about from the ways you save costs for your customers, expand their revenues, and enhance their capabilities to be competitively advantaged.

Validating a Service Concept

If you canvass your current customer base to ask them if they would do business with you as a provider of a service, you will end up deceiving yourself. It costs nothing, nor does it profit you anything, for them to say yes. The only way to validate a service business concept is to challenge customers with a business proposition based on the competitive advantage it can provide. Then they will know its costs and their benefits.

Here is a reduced cost that a 30 percent shorter downtime cycle can contribute to your manufacturing, you must be able to say. Compare it to your current cost of downtime. If the improvement we propose is significant, ask us how we can help you achieve it. We will tell you whether we propose to better integrate some or all of the components of your current manufacturing process, reengineer it, or manage your manufacturing process with you or for you, either in whole or in part.

We will show you how we have arrived at the return you will receive on your investment with us, when you will achieve payback, and how the annual cash flows will add up over a three-year commercial life cycle. We will then recommend how you can reinvest a portion of your savings with us to lengthen the meantime between downtimes so that your profit contribution from manufacturing can be further increased by an additional 30 to 40 percent.

For a dealer or distributor customer in a consumer products business, you must be able to say something like this: Here is an increased stream of revenues that can contribute an annual increment of $1 million to a major category of your business. Compare it to your current revenues. If the improvement we propose is significant, ask us how we can help you achieve it. We will tell you whether we propose to better integrate some or all of your warehousing systems, reengineer them, or manage your inventory functions with you or for you, either in whole or in part.

We will show you how we have arrived at the return you will receive on your investment with us, when you will achieve payback, and how the annual cash flows will add up over a three-year commercial life cycle. We will then recommend how you can reinvest a portion of your earnings with us to add another 20 percent to your annual profit contribution from improved inventory management.

Services are validated by their results. Since service businesses relate to their clients as fiduciary stewards, service results must be accounted for in financial terms. To be a business advisor in a service sense means to be an investment advisor who proposes "good deals" whose goodness is proved on their bottom lines. A service is only as good as its deals. It may be known by the clients it keeps, but it keeps its clients by continuous deals to improve their profitability.

Validating a service is validating its profit-making power. The "how" of a service is always secondary to its "how much" because the "how much" is what its clients buy and what they pay for. If they were asked to pay for the "how," which is your capability base and the processes by which you implement it, they would convert it into a product and ask you to discount its price.

Knowledge-Basing Your Service

Product-based businesses recite a mantra that reminds them to "know the customer's business." But what they usually know is how their customers buy, not how they make profits from what they buy. They know how a customer operates the business function that does his purchasing, but they have little to no knowledge of how the customer operates his business as a whole.

Data shock awaits managers who fail to acknowledge this distinction. As they make the transition from being product-based to a service, they realize that most of what they know about their customers is either inadequate or irrelevant. As soon as a customer becomes a client who must be grown instead of sold to, it is no longer sufficient to know who buys your products, who influences your buyers, and what their "personal wins" are that you may be able to enhance.

• If you are going to provide a service to improve the profit contribution of client manufacturing operations, you must know things that you may never have known before: each client's current reject rate and how you can reduce it at the greatest cost savings and increase in productivity, and how much of an impact your improvements make on shipments, billings, and receivable collections. The same degree of finite quantified knowledge holds true for downtime rates and cycles, rework rates performed under warranty, and recalls.

• If you are going to provide a service to improve the profit contribution of supermarket client operations, you must know a good deal more than your optimal price points and competitive share points. You must be able to quantify each client's optimal mix of your products and competitive products in your category, the relative added values to each client of your couponing compared to 2-for-1 promotions and cents-off deals, and the reduced cost contributions that can be made by your stockless inventory plans and just-in-time deliveries.

Without these types of data, you will be unable to apply your service expertise because you will have no adequate knowledge of what you must apply it to.

Service markets are applications markets. The value of a transaction to a service client is directly proportional to its outcome. Service clients pay for what they get out of your service, not what you have put into it in the forms of the hourly rates of your applications experts or the manufactured costs of your products. These inputs may have little or no relation to your clients' outcomes from their application.

If you are going to manage a service business, it will do you no good to have the best product if it does not make a measurably better incremental contribution to a client's competitiveness than the next-best product. If your pride and your passion are in manufacturing the best product rather than applying it with the best expertise using the best knowledge of the customer's business, you will be bringing a product mindset to a service business. If nothing else alerts you, your margins will.

Service businesses evaluate their products according to their "good-enoughness." The product components of a service must be good enough to maximize their contribution to customer competitiveness. They cannot be less than good enough. Nor do they need to be more. The good-enoughness test evaluates product quality and performance according to customer contribution. This means that what your customers need to get out of what you make determines what you put in. Anything less or noncontributory will negatively affect customer satisfaction with you. Anything more will negatively affect your cost-effectiveness as a service business. You will have to be a higher cost provider or give your margins away to stay competitive. One of the most important categories of customer data you will have to know is each customer's definition of *good enough*.

Clients are the ultimate quality controllers of service businesses. They will set your product specifications for you. Where do I find the extra value you put in? they will ask you. In what part of my operation—is it in a lower cost here or improved cash flow there? How much is it in proportion to my total value? If I cannot find its contribution or it is disproportional to its added cost, why are you putting it in? Why am I paying for it?

The applications markets of service businesses are far more information intensive and education intensive than product-performance intensive. The knowledge that comes with a product—how to implement it most cost-effectively —is the accelerator of its value. This makes service businesses and their markets data dependent.

In assessing your market opportunity for a service business, the question, *How much can we teach its customers?* is a key discriminator of your potential market vitality. The question gets to the heart of a market's need for your applications expertise to improve its competitiveness: What can we teach customers about maximizing the contributions to profits made by their major operations? The more there is for you to teach, the more there will be for you to sell at high margins.

Suppose you are the Consumer Products Division of 3M and you sell to Kmart. Where do your products go when you sell them? Some of them go into Kmart's stationery departments. What does Kmart do in this function of its business that 3M may be able to help them do better, do differently, or do more cost-effectively, either cheaper or more productively? In order to teach Kmart how its profits can be improved, 3M will have to know where Kmart's main costs cluster in doing business with 3M and where Kmart's main revenue improvement opportunities can occur from doing more business or doing different business or doing business differently with 3M.

3M and Kmart need to put their heads together to access two types of data:

1. What it currently costs Kmart to do business with 3M that 3M and Kmart can manage better. The three questions that 3M must ask Kmart to get at this data are shown in Figure 2-4.
2. What it currently yields Kmart to do business with 3M that 3M and Kmart can manage better. The three questions that 3M must ask Kmart to get at this data are shown in Figure 2-5.

When 3M gets into Kmart's business with it, 3M may discover inventory and distribution functions that 3M can comanage or manage for Kmart. 3M may also discover new product and promotion opportunities. For each one, how much will Kmart be able to save? How much more will Kmart earn? What will the cost and revenue impacts be on 3M?

Bumper-Stickering Service Guidelines

Competitive disadvantage or insufficient advantage is everywhere in the businesses of your customers. All of them have one or the other. Wherever advantage exists today, it is

Figure 2-4. What it costs Kmart to do business with 3M.

---

1. When Kmart 80-20s its costs of doing business with 3M, what are the 20 percent of 3M practices and policies that account for 80 percent of the total 3M contribution?

   1.1. What categories of costs?
   1.2. How much do they amount to?

2. When Kmart compares its costs of doing business with 3M to its costs with other suppliers, how does 3M rank?

   2.1. Where is 3M the costliest supplier or among the costliest suppliers?
   2.2. By how much?

3. Which of these cost categories are on Kmart's "must list" to reduce?

---

transient. It needs to be managed—to be "serviced" in order to stretch it out as long as possible and then enhance it.

Unless your clients grow in advantage as a result of the service you provide, you have provided them with no service. They will have failed to receive the value they paid for in the form of the profits you proposed to improve for them. As a matter of fact, you will actually have disserved them by costing them the time value of an opportunity to grow that is impossible for them to reclaim.

On the value chain of the 1990s, products have the lowest value because, in and of themselves, they are essentially dumb. They await animation by application and the ability to contribute to customer growth through consultation, education, and information. Unanimated and uninformed by either human or artificial intelligence, products remain inert costs.

At the customer's end of the value chain, management services carry the greatest worth. They put products to work in an expertly controlled smart environment that ensures the maximum yield of each product's benefits. This is the ultimate service because it touches a client's business at the points where value is expected to be created by his own business managers and the managers of his business functions.

This is one of three guidelines to transform a product business into a service: Instead of selling products to customer buyers, provide a service for customer managers. A second guideline has to do with your focus. Instead of concentrating on the control of your own manufacturing and marketing processes, focus on improving your customers' controls. Third, integrate your objectives with the objectives of your customers. Instead of just trying to be your industry's low-cost producer or market-share leader, try to help your custom-

Figure 2-5. What it yields Kmart to do business with 3M.

---

1. When Kmart 80-20s its revenues from doing business with 3M, what are the 20 percent of 3M products that account for 80 percent of the total 3M contribution?

    1.1. What product lines?
    1.2. How much do the revenues amount to? How much of the revenues are earnings?

2. When Kmart compares its revenues and earnings from doing business with 3M to its revenues and earnings from other suppliers, how does 3M rank?

    2.1. Where is 3M their revenue or earnings leader or among the leaders?
    2.2. By how much?

3. Which of these revenue and earnings categories are on Kmart's "must list" to expand?

---

ers be among their own industries' low-cost producers and market-share leaders.

If you want to be sure that these principles of service stick with your people, you can distill them into shaving-mirror injunctions like these:

- Help each customer make his numbers. In return, he will help you make yours.
- Grow each customer's managers. In return, they will grow you.

3

How to Develop the
Key Service Skill
of Consulting

Consultation is the hinge skill between being a product-based business and becoming a service. It is the delivery system for a service provider's expertise, the engine that drives the contributions that a service makes to its clients' enhanced competitiveness.

The consultant's mission is spelled out in Figure 3-1. IBM says it somewhat differently, stating that the mission of its consultants is to delight their customers by understanding their business requirements, "consistently delivering high quality, integrated technology solutions and service offerings, and always providing unfailing, exceptional support." This statement reveals that IBM is still at the technology-oriented product end of the value chain.

IBM's mission puts technology solutions first, followed by service and support in the traditional product-based rank order. This will make it difficult for IBM's consultants to "exceed customer expectations," their ultimate objective. Integrated technology solutions delight no one except technology consultants. Business consultants do their paired dances of delight with their clients at the teller's windows of their banks, not in the "glass houses" of their management information systems.

Business consultants have three distinguishing characteristics:

1. They never tell you how much better they are than
   their competitors. Instead, they tell you how much
   better their clients are than the companies that com-
   pete against them. If they are really good, they let their
   clients testify for them.
2. They never ask you to give them unilateral information. Instead, they share their knowledge with you in
   a way that teaches you something about how you can
   help improve your business. At the same time, it
   teaches you what they need to know more about in
   order for you to realize the benefits of their help.
3. They never try to tell you how to run your business.
   Instead, they propose alternate strategies to help you
   run it better. Working within your objectives, they
   propose ways to achieve them faster and with greater
   certainty or even exceed them.

A consultant's standards of performance are met when
the incremental profit objectives of each project that he or she
manages are met within their predicted time frame so that
customer satisfaction is maximized and the implementation of
the next planned project can begin with minimum downtime.

Client profit improvement must be continuous. There
must never be a time when a consultant is not contributing
incremental growth to his clients. Downtime represents unaffordable opportunity costs to both of them. It also leaves the
consultant exposed to competitive inroads by inviting the
answer "nothing" to the question, What have you done for
me lately? The best policy is for each consultant-client partnership always to have one project on the table, the next one
heating up in the oven, and the next one after that in the
freezer awaiting defrosting.

The sequencing of a consultant's work is a function of
joint growth planning with each client. A joint growth plan
schedules, funds, and integrates their work together so that

Figure 3-1. Consultant position description.

CONSULTANTS sell money, not products. They transact returns from investments, not sales. Their price is an investment, not a cost. Their performance is measured by the amount and rate of the customer's return, not product performance benefits. They work inside their customer businesses as partners, not from the outside as vendors. They relate directly to customer business-function managers and profit center managers, not purchasing agents. They work at these middle management levels on a long-term, continuing basis, not from bid to bid. Their focus is not on competitive suppliers, but on competitive profit making for their customer partners and for themselves.

first things are done first and that each cycle of migrations from them follows in logical extension.

Being Driven by Client Rights

A consultant's position description can be deduced from his standards of performance. Consultants plan, implement, and measure their clients' incremental growth. In one word, they must be *growers*. The value they add over and above the already planned growth of their clients determines their worth and serves as the basis for their reward. As a consultant grows his clients, they grow him. This is the win-win platform for consulting.

The joint planning process is a consultant's bond with his clients. It ensures the mutual commitment of sufficient resources to achieve each objective and, at the same time, acknowledges that neither the consultant nor his client can realize the objectives they plan without the other. The plan is the final arbiter of the two unasked questions about which all clients must be presumed to speculate: Can I do as well by myself? Can I do even better with another consultant?

Consultants must be client-driven. You cannot be a consultant unless you know what it must be like to be your client: It must be comfortable, it must be a learning experience, and it must yield measurable, quantifiable results.

A client is not just a customer gussied up with eye shadow and lip rouge. Clienthood endows a customer with certain inalienable rights that can be called the "rights of clienthood." They are the consultant's trade-offs—the values he must give in return for the value of the high margins he receives. A client's rights should become a consultant's standard operating procedure. Along with improving client profits, recognizing client rights while doing so is the *sine qua non* of consulting.

Some of the more important client rights include the following:

- *Cure me.* Get things done. Anticipate my needs. Produce results fast because I have more needs.

- *Speak my language.* Talk profit improvement and competitive advantage. Make your points in businessese, not tech-talk.
- *No surprises.* Plan our work and work our plan. Measure and monitor everything we do together.
- *Level with me.* Tell it like it is. Don't fudge facts or perpetuate fictions.
- *Play on my team.* Be around. Ask questions. Share my objectives.
- *Teach me.* Let me learn from you. Train my people to implement your expertise.
- *Take leadership.* Get out in front of situations. Get your hands dirty in our operations.
- *Worry for me.* Think about my problems. Give me access to you when I am worried.
- *Be creative.* Give me something new. Make me stand out.
- *Be flexible.* Give in from time to time, but don't ever give up. Yield on methods and means but not on our goals.

Applying Management Expertise

A consultant's job can be described like this:

- To improve his client's profits
- In a partnered working relationship
- By applying the added value of his expertise to solve a client business problem or seize a client business opportunity
- So that the client gains a competitive advantage that is measurably greater than his investment in the consultant's service

The profit improvement of a client is the consultant's number one job. Its performance is judged by a comparison of two sets of values: the value of client costs reduced or the value of client revenues expanded compared against the value of the client's investment in the consultant.

Applying managerial expertise is the process by which a consultant improves a client's profits. The consultant process itself follows a four-step agenda, as Figure 3-2 shows. First, a consultant analyzes an opportunity; second, he posits a solution; third, he gains agreement that it is the single best solution; and fourth, he manages or comanages a project that

Figure 3-2. Consultant process.

---

1. *Analyze the opportunity.* Impose your experience on a customer's situation to discover his needs, which will show up as deviations from your norms. Once you target a need, make sure you have a corrective fit that will solve it in a cost-effective manner. Write up the need in the form of a "finding."

2. *Posit the solution.* Calculate the most cost-effective solution to help the customer more closely approach your norms. Write up the solution on an "if-then" basis, so that the deliverables become your "recommendations" of the results to be expected from the time and resources that will be expended.

3. *Agree on the solution.* Gain agreement that your solution is the single best solution to achieve the objective of bringing the customer closer to your norms.

4. *Manage the project.* Make a joint action plan to schedule the partnered realization of the solution according to progressive milestones of achievement. Attach a measurement and monitor system to evaluate results at each milestone to ensure maintaining the predicted balance between time and money costs and their benefits. Implement the next migration immediately.

---

will implement the solution in the timeliest and most cost-effective manner.

There are three pressure points in the consultant's process. The first comes just before step one. It is to gain access to the client's data. The second comes just before step two. It is to get to proposal. The third comes just after step four. It is to get to solution, with its migration to the next recycling of the process already built in.

Companies that are adopting consultation as the "point strategy" in their transformation to a service are giving their consultants a variety of names, among them, relationship managers, client executives, and opportunity managers.

They are being positioned "to provide advice and counsel on strategic direction and on how businesses can be operated better using our technologies so that clients can increase their long-term strengths and improve their market shares."

Consultants are being given ownership of their client relationships, being held responsible as well as accountable for the mutual profitability and customer satisfaction of their partnerships. On their authority, the full resource capabilities of their companies, and any other suppliers, can be committed to develop and implement client solutions. Working within cross-function teams, consultants will focus on dedicated market segments such as retail banking or consumer packaged goods or hospitals so that they can become industry experts who represent their industry's standards for competitive advantage.

Avoiding Wrong Reasons

Businesses that base their prices on product performance and base their performance standards on product features and benefits make a fetish of "staying close" to their customers. When they do, however, they generally use their closeness to improve their own products and processes instead of improving the profit contributions they can make to customer products and processes. They mistake closeness for consultation.

Consultants are distinguished by a raised consciousness to their clients' prosperity. They think remedially about the client costs and revenues that determine competitiveness. They know that they cannot afford to allow a client to remain noncompetitive. If they do, the client loses the benefits of the consultant's solutions while the consultant loses the client. As partners, either they grow together or they will forfeit their mutual opportunities.

Companies that use staying close to the advantage of their own products rather than their customers' competitiveness will learn about consulting from companies that use staying close to the advantage of their clients. They will learn the hard way that one of the main rules for doing business in the 1990s will be "consult or be consulted to."

You must be careful not to be attracted to consulting for the wrong reasons. Many companies see consulting as a device to sell to top-level customer managers where their product sales representatives cannot penetrate. For IBM, consulting has become a way "to enhance our relationship with customers at the senior executive level." These relationships had gone out of style for IBM when its hardware and software became commodity products. As a result, senior customers had been delegating purchase decisions as far down as possible in their organizations. The "gee whiz" access that IBM had traditionally merited to customers' executive suites had become severely limited.

By the use of consultants, companies like IBM want to create strong, long-term relationships with their senior customers who may be able to exert substantial influence in recommending products. Instead of selling consultation as a premium service, they are willing to trade small consulting revenues from the top where they have little or nothing to sell for the possibility that increased product business may flow down to them through the customer organization.

With this bastardization of consulting as a loss leader, they compound the existing margin problems of their product-based businesses. Their hope is to gain higher revenues from increased sales, followed by even greater revenue opportunities from follow-on product support, implementation,

tion, and education services once they get their foot in the door.

To carry out this type of foreshortened mission for consulting, companies that use its powers in order to sell products permit themselves to settle for a watered-down definition of their consultants. They look for people who are "responsive and helpful" when they need assertive people who take the initiative in solving client problems instead of merely being responsive to them. They look for people who are "willing to share risk" instead of people who can rule out risk as a client constraint. They look for people who can "take ownership of customer problems" instead of people who can own or co-own client facilities so that problems can be preempted at their source.

Keeping Products Secret

In order to craft a consulting hinge for transforming your business to a service, you will have to adopt selling strategies that are largely unknown to product sellers and may even be unimagined by them.

• You will have to be able to approach Procter & Gamble's brand managers, not their purchasing managers, and propose to add the incremental dollar values of reduced costs and increased revenues from each promotion for their products. If you sell a software product to realize these values, the product will remain your secret until you have established your ability to add to your client's values.

• You will have to be able to approach General Dynamics' project managers, not their technopurchasing or information systems managers, and propose to add the incremental dollar values of increased product throughput, reduced downtime and increased meantime between downtimes, and a reduced rate of rejects compared to shippable products. If you sell a test and measurement system to realize these values, the product will remain your secret until you have established your ability to add to your client's values.

• You will have to be able to approach McDonald's top-level managers and propose to add to the revenues and earnings being contributed by their best stores. Your single best solution will be to develop and implement an ever-normal forecasting and inventory control system that will reduce to zero their out-of-stock problem with the fastest moving, highest margin products. You will bundle your consultant's compensation into McDonald's total investment with you. You will base the amount of the investment on the incremental revenues and earnings you propose to add. You will guarantee them. If you sell a computer system to realize these values, the system will remain your secret until you have established your ability to add to your client's values.

If you manufacture a product, teach your consultants to keep it in the car. If they do not have a plan to propose added value to their clients, teach them to stay in the car until they do. If they do not know how to quantify their added value, make them return the car until they promise never to leave home without knowing how.

Consultative Selling, the sales strategy that has been specifically designed for consultants, is based on the premise that what you put on the table when you go before a customer must be the single deliverable that will add your value to him. The value you add will become the basis for your price, and therefore the source of your margins. A product alone will never suffice. Nor will a service alone. As soon as it is put on the table by itself, it will be priced like a product. The only element that can merit premium margins is the benefit of the consultant's installed value. Everything else is a cost. This is why nothing other than the consultant's value, not the consultant's time or talents, should ever be sold.

Facing the Verities

Consulting is done in numbers, not in words. Consultants who try to narrate client growth end up talking to themselves. Clients have ears and balance sheets only for numbers. In both cases, each dollar of improved profits is worth a thousand words. The only truth in consulting is "in the numbers." The concept of "a lot" means whatever anybody wants it to mean, but a client can always locate $2 million exactly equidistant between $1 million and $3 million and can then decide for himself whether or not it is a lot.

Numbers that express the dollar value and time value of a client's profit improvement are a consultant's steak. Everything else is parsley. If consultants can be said to have a universal motto, it would be "More dollars sooner" for their clients.

Words obscure numbers. What they do not obscure, they qualify. Consultants bearing words instead of numbers are shirking commitment. They are refusing to commit to a value that their expertise should enable them to add to a client. When this occurs, they are confessing that they have nothing to consult about.

There is no place for words at a client's top line where cash flows are found nor at his bottom line where profits accrue. If the numbers are there, words are superfluous. If the numbers are not there, words are also superfluous.

The verities of consulting are all dollar truths. When a client asks, How do we get there from here? a consultant must deal with three sets of dollar truths:

1. How much cost or revenue flow is associated with "here"?
2. How much less cost or how much more revenue flow is associated with "there"?
3. How much will have to be invested for how long to get there from here?

A consultant's objectives are money goals. His strategies for achieving the objectives are costs, which are negative dollar values. Since strategies represent a special classification of costs known as investments, time values must also enter into a consultant's numbers. When will a client's investment be repaid and when will full realization of its return be in hand?

Because consultants trade off positive returns for client investments, consulting is a brokering function. Consultants do deals. Their equivalent of the broker's "Do I have a deal for you!" is somewhat more complex but recognizably similar:

"What if this business function or line of business of yours can be helped to make an improved contribution to your profits by $1.5 million within the next 12 months—is that significant enough for you to ask me *how*?" By asking *how?* the consultant's client opens the deal.

Without facing the verities of consulting that enable you to define your business as a service, you are going to have nothing but margin problems no matter how good your products are. Motorola has learned this the hard way. Even when Motorola helps to write customer specifications for its Smartnet portable radiotelephone systems, the customers can still get "very excited about the capabilities and prices" of its competitor Ericsson/GE. This occurs in spite of the fact that since 1928, "Motorola has been providing the world with superb electronic products that illustrate our companywide values: creative research, rigorous testing, meticulous production and outstanding service—all contributing to our ultimate goal of customer satisfaction."

If Motorola were a service business, its clients—not Motorola—would be illustrating its companywide values in testimonial case histories like this: "Motorola consultants have been providing us with outstanding competitive advantages in $3.5 million of reduced costs, $1.25 million from improved productivity, $11 million of expanded sales, and $1.5 million of enhanced profits. As a result, we have been able to set new industry standards for the operations that Motorola consultants help us manage."

Motorola is typical of product-based companies that put one foot tentatively forward in the direction of their customers but keep all of their corporate weight well back on the other foot. "We don't want to simply manufacture radios," Motorola says. "We want to design radio communications systems to meet your individual business needs." But without a consultative capability, these needs may turn out to be tied to ineffective and inefficient customer operations. What compelling competitive advantage can come of simply improving communications?

What if work crews are wrongly allocated by the way a construction industry customer operates? What if they are so poorly managed that they sit around waiting for inexpertly scheduled materials to be delivered to a work site? Who will integrate the customer's current system, reengineer its work flows, or step forward and offer to manage it better? Who will be able to say to the customer, "You are construction managers. We manage communications for construction businesses. Under our management, businesses like yours can reduce their labor costs by an average 20 to 30 percent and your materials costs by an additional 10 percent. The average project can be completed 15 to 20 days sooner, allowing you to bill up to half a month earlier and reallocate your resources to the next project. If these improved contributions to your profit per project are significant to you, ask us how we can engineer, integrate, and manage a customized communications network for you."

Motorola knows that its construction customers lose control of their operations from time to time to the detriment of their costs and cash flows. In order to meet their needs to maintain control, Motorola has been moving up the value scale from being wholly product based in "simply manufacturing radios" to more of a service posture in "designing radio communications systems." But Motorola still has a way to go as a service.

"You are misallocating too many of your workers," Motorola must be able to say. "As a result, your productivity per worker is too low. Their downtimes are too frequent and last too long. You do not turn them over fast enough from one project to the next. Therefore, you are unlikely to meet your strategic plans." But without consultative capabilities, there will be no one at Motorola who can make these statements.

Enhancing Client Plans

Consultants are strategic enhancers, not strategic planners. Strategic plans are client responsibilities. Consultants must accelerate the achievement of a client's plan or increase its overall value by targeting the smallest number of objectives to which they can contribute the greatest improvements in the shortest amounts of time.

This requires consultants to be plan-literate. Otherwise, they will replicate the experience of the joint venture between Hewlett-Packard and Northern Telecom. The venture's consultants offered to network the combined data processing and telecommunications strategies of major corporations in advance of planned corporate growth so that their state-of-the-art in information technology would always be ahead of their business needs. Show us your growth plans, the venturers said. But none of the venturers could read them.

Reading a client's strategic business plans means two things. One is the ability to identify its crunch points, the 20 percent or fewer of the critical factors that will determine up to 80 percent of its success. The other is the ability to target 80 percent of your capabilities to add value from the client's 20 percent. This is where a consultant's expertise comes into play. It tells him where to look and what to look for in each industry he knows: the key cost centers whose burdens he can help reduce the most and the key revenue centers whose ability to generate funds he can help expand the most.

If a consultant can preempt these key opportunities to improve client profits—key because of their importance to his clients and because he can make important contributions to them—his clients will find him compelling. They will be compelled to bring him in.

Consultants must know what they are looking at and what they are looking for. Where client costs are higher than they should be, resources are being needlessly overcommitted. Where a client's intensities of labor or materials are too great, or operating cycle times are too long, capabilities are being duplicated or they have been allowed to lag technology.

Where client revenues or earnings are lower than they should be, markets are being underserved or margins are being overly discounted, products have been allowed to become obsolescent to the point where they have lost their differentiation or traditional distribution channels may need to be bypassed.

A consultant compares a customer's planned or actual utilization of his asset base with what he knows to be optimal levels of utilization. He or she then prescribes a project to optimize the customer's assets. The project may prescribe a better integration of the operation as it stands, a reengineering of the operation, or management of the customer's operation by the consultant. The economic benefits of the prescription become the consultant's "product."

Product-based companies work the other way around. They put their product's cart before the consultant's horse, as Asea Brown Boveri does when it says that "The associated benefit of improving a customer's product quality is realizing the economic advantage that can be obtained." If ABB led its business with a consultative capability instead of a process-based capability, it would know that the customer's economic advantage is the prime advantage. Improved product quality is an associated benefit that contributes to it.

"Here is your enhanced return from savings on a more optimal mix of materials, labor, and energy in your process," ABB consultants would be able to say. "Here are the enhanced revenues from improved product quality and production efficiencies. And here is the optimized process we are prescribing for you to realize these enhanced economic and production values—one of which is improved product quality—that will help you fulfill your strategic plan or exceed it."

Managing Expert Power

Consultants have a single source of power: the power of the expert. At the outset of each engagement, consultants may possess proprietary information, strategic scenarios or technology that their clients do not know, and this will give them some transient knowledge power. But the only enduring power for a consultant is the expert ability to apply what he knows to what he learns about a client's operations.

Clients look to a consultant to apply expert power in three ways:

1. As resident technical expert who can internalize his skills, systems, and strategies by customizing their application to fit the way client people work.
2. As teacher who can train client people to apply his skills, systems, and strategies so that they become institutionalized as the client's own standards of performance.
3. As project manager who can plan, process, and prove his solutions in partnership with client teams.

As Figure 3-3 shows, these three roles draw upon a mix of management, technical, and interpersonal skills. A consultant must use them to manage the two scarce resources of time and money. While managing each profit project, the consultant much coach and counsel his customer partners in the transfer of his tools, methods, and standards so they can become internalized. The consultant must prepare the logical extension of each project into its successive migrations to ensure the continuity and consistency of his profit improvement plans. And all the time, he must make it challenging for each client to be his partner in profit improvement even if, for him, it is old hat because he has done it dozens of times before. For his client partners, it will always be their first time. Their shock of discovery at each "ah-hah moment" should be paramount among their rewards from the consultant experience.

Selling Subjectivity

If you run an unsophisticated consultancy, you will make a fetish of a consultant's objectivity. You will say that a consultant must come fresh to each client problem or opportunity unfettered by preconceptions, preferences, or his or her own products. If you say these things, you will be negating a

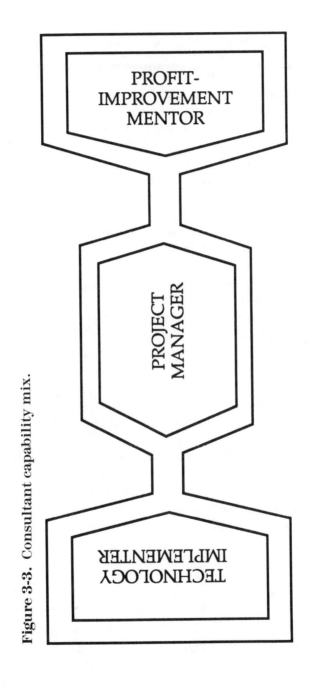

Figure 3-3. Consultant capability mix.

63

consultant's most precious possession, the biases of his or her experience.

Innocent consultants are consultants without experience or the freedom to use it. Subjectivity, not objectivity, is the sum of all the lessons learned in the school of hard knocks where the curriculum is composed of what works and what does not work. Objectivity is virginity. Subjectivity is expert power, the strength of a point of view about what enhances a client strategy most cost-effectively to make it more competitively advantaged.

A subjective consultant—the phrase is tautological, needlessly repetitive—is positioned with a built-in strategic slant. He stands for it. Slant predisposes the consultant to have a personal vision of an optimal outcome and a preconceived set of preferred strategies that must be customized to fit each client's specific situation.

A consultant's preference must be in favor of the solution that his experience has taught him will be the single best solution as long as he can get positive answers to questions like these:

- Is the client's specific situation analogous to past situations where I am experienced in successfully implementing this solution?
- Is the situation free from pernicious contraries that could negate my experience?
- Is the situation free from requiring the addition of innovative components to the solution that could significantly alter its cost-effectiveness or my confidence in its applicability?

Consultants should wear their subjectivity on their sleeves: "This is what I believe, this is what I stand for—*these outcomes* from *this solution* implemented with *these strategies* within *this time frame*. Every system I install will be customized. But no system I install will be beyond the range of my experience in what works best. The single best solution I prescribe to implement with you will be one with which I am comfortable, confident, and competent."

Subjectivity is more than what a consultant stands for in terms of strategic ideology. It is also what he will not stand for in the way of extraneous strategies that he fears will dilute or pollute his successful implementation.

Pricing the Consultant's Contribution

If you bring your product-selling heritage with you into consulting, you will be tempted to corrupt the service nature of consultation with product vending habits. You will make consultation a product, put a cost-plus price on its man-hours, and end up discounting it the same way that products are discounted. By selling a service like a product, you will cause its margins to flee from it because an hour of consulting time is an hour just as a personal computer is a personal computer, polypropylene is polypropylene, and an oil field drill bit is a drill bit.

You will have commoditized what must be a branded service if it is to command high margins.

Consulting strategies that sell time by the hour base their price on their cost, not their value. The value of an hour should be based on how it is applied to solving a problem or realizing an opportunity in a customer's business. No two hours have the same value even though they may be charged out at the same cost. A lower-costed hour may have greater value than a higher-costed hour; their contributions to value may be inversely proportional. It is the dollar value of the customer costs that are reduced or the customer revenues that are expanded that determines each hour's value. If a million dollars of costs can be reduced or an equal amount of revenues can be increased in an hour, is the worth of the hour predicated on its cost or its applied value?

Pricing for consulting services is not a lost art; it is an as yet unfound one for most transformed businesses. Few consultants measure the value of their advice. Even fewer would know how to charge for it beyond adding "something on" to their costs. All sorts of formulas abound. One of them sums up the total book prices of the products that a consultant sells, adds a percentage for time costs and a pinch of "value pricing," which turns out to be an uneducated quess. Very few product-based businesses that "get into" consulting have the nerve to throw away their price books, throw in their products for free, and assess a fee in proportion to the net value of the customer costs they can reduce or the revenues they can help to expand.

Hourly rates for consultation are death to margins. They invite customers to shop for lower rates, either from a more junior consultant or an alternate vendor of consulting services. Value-based management fees, in contrast, can be positioned as customer investments instead of costs. They can be sold on the basis of their return, to which they will appear small by comparison. This is the first comparison that should be made. The second comparison is to relate the improved outcome from consultation to the current cost or revenue stream: the new reduced customer cost versus the original cost or the new enlarged stream of revenues versus the original revenues. The difference between the outcome and the original costs or revenues equals the value added by consultation.

Jones, Day, Reavis & Pogue has found the magic formula. The law firm has spun out its consulting services as an affiliate called Innovative Strategies in order to value-base its fee structure per project rather than be saddled by the lawyers' traditional hourly billing rates. The affiliate is also open to royalty payments.

Selling on Value

All consultation should always be priced on performance, not the cost of the performer. This provides the consultant's incentive. It also provides the client's rationale for investing in the consultant's services.

By selling on value, consultants become sellers of an investment's return. They remove the concept of cost from the buying equation. Consultants should never be a cost to their clients; paying for a consultant's service should be investing in an addition of value to the operation being served. The consultant's answer to the question, How much do you charge? should be *nothing*. The answer to the question, How do you get paid? should be *as a share of the return we achieve on our mutual investment*. When a consultant can be perceived as a co-investor of his own talents and resources— including his time—he can be accepted as an equal partner in a joint enterprise with his client. When this occurs, the consultant's customer becomes a client. The objective of their joint enterprise is mutual profit improvement.

A consultant's management fees are his reward for managing an allocation of his client's human and financial resources in such a way that their value is enhanced. This gives a consultant fiduciary responsibility as a caretaker of his client's wealth, investing it for maximum gain commensurate with early payback and reasonable risk. When a consultant shares his clients' risk, he is entitled to share in their reward.

Undervaluing consulting services leads to underpricing them. Discounting consulting services leads to further undervaluing them. The combination of underpricing and discounting takes all the juice out of their margin power. Under an all-court press for services—IBM chairman John Akers has said that half of IBM's total revenues must come from services by the end of the decade—IBM's service revenues grew 35 percent in 1991. But the gross profit margin on services was only 18.8 percent, almost a third lower than for IBM as a whole.

The formula for successful pricing of consultant services is PV > PP: a consultant's *premium value* must always be greater than his *premium price*. The higher the value premium, the higher the price can be as long as the value still exceeds it. It is important to note that the formula's driver is premium *value*, not premium product *performance*. Premium performance drives low-margin vendor sales and is the hallmark of commodity products rather than branded consultant services.

As you plan your transformation into a service business, your focus should be on maximizing the PV component in the consultant's pricing formula. This will lead you to develop an applications-intensive business strategy. The consultation, information, implementation, and education that your consultants provide will be the key ingredients in helping your clients to manage their current assets more profitably and to grow new assets.

Branding Service Margins

The quality of your consultants' applications technology is the most important contributor to your business as a service. It must exceed even the technical excellence of your products. The formula for the optimal allocation of your internal assets to ensure applications primacy is PAT > PPT: *Premium applications technology* must always be greater than *premium product technology.* If you reverse the formula, you will revert to a product-based business. If you have to make a choice, it will be helpful to consider the formula in these terms: Customer competitiveness can be better served by superior applications expertise coupled to a parity product than by a superior product constrained by parity applications expertise, implementation, education, and consultation.

The consultant's role is to maximize the return from allocating your assets to the client assets where they can do the most good in maximizing return for both of you. This is known as asset management. Each consultant's acid test as an asset manager will be his or her answer to the single most crucial question: *Are You Getting Your Margins?*

Unless a consultant succeeds in branding his value, he will not be able to command his margins. A consultant's brandable value is the result of his application skills. These are areas of expertise that define the ability of their provider to put his value to work for each of his clients in such a client-specific manner that it yields its maximum rated capacity to improve client profits.

Brandedness and its relation to high margins can be reduced to a general doctrine, as Figure 3-4 shows. The doctrine is composed of two parts. One obtains agreement on the purpose of branding. The other sets guidelines for affixing a premium price to your brand. A brand doctrine can help

Figure 3-4. Brand doctrine.

Agreements on Brand Purpose

1. Our prime objective is profit growth.
2. Our prime purpose in growing profits is to be self-financing in our ability to generate capital.
3. Our prime means of profit growth is to command high unit margins.
4. Our prime strategy for commanding high margins is to create specialty, proprietary, and performance types of services that deliver high added value to our customers.

Guidelines to Branded Pricing

1. A brand's ability to deliver high value determines its ability to command a high margin.
2. A brand's value-to-price ratio must always favor value so that it is perceived to be a bargain when its returned value is compared to the price invested to achieve it.
3. A brand's price is never listed since it varies directly with its associated value.
4. A brand's price and value are reciprocal. Its price certifies its value and its value bases its price.

---

make brand building everybody's business in your organization so that the mean times before maturity for the value of each of your business life cycles can be stretched out as long as possible.

When you plan the sales of a service you have branded, you have two types of strategies at your disposal for making money:

    1. Keep your *price* as high as possible in order to maximize your profits on sales.

2. Keep your investment in *assets employed* as low as possible in order to minimize your costs of sales.

In a service business, your primary branding irons are people—the consultants who implement your installations and applications and who inform and educate your clients.

Brand prices resist standardization. Each investment will vary in direct proportion to each client's return. Since the return is the consultant's "product," and since no two "products" are ever the same, no two prices can ever be the same either. In this respect, service businesses are always custom providers. A consultant with a price list is a vendor in consultant's clothing.

Consultants are perceived as high priced or overpriced only when their value is perceived to be less than their fee; that is, when the investment required to retain them seems to exceed its return. The faster the return is realized, the greater the consultant's value. When clients receive an early payback on their investment in a consultant's service, their payout amounts to giving a short-term loan to the consultant to manage. A consultant who proves himself to be a reliable manager of customer funds—who turns them over quickly at the predicted rate of profit—becomes literally "priceless."

Taking Up Residence

Consulting achieves its maximum value when a consultant is retained, not engaged. Retainers tend to be longer term than engagements, giving a consultant tenure in his client relationships that permits him to be accepted into partnership. As partners, consultants and their clients are married. If consultants sell periodic projects instead of continuous partnered profit improvement, they will never be more than engaged.

Tenured consultants can work at the highest end of the value chain because they operate at the highest end of their learning curve about a client's problems and opportunities. They know each client's business as an insider. They know its critical success factors. They know its principal players who, in turn, have tested the consultant's value and are comfortable with partnering him or her to obtain it. Knowing the consultant's value, they can rationalize his fees.

Consulting services that sell short-term projects are, in effect, selling a product here and now and another product there and then. Each engagement requires a separate proposal as its entry fee; there is a beginning and an end to it, and when it is over there is no assurance that a new engagement will be forthcoming. In a partnership, each successive project is proposed while the consultant is under retainer; consequently, he is being paid to propose his client's next investment opportunity. As client funds must be continuously invested if they are to grow and, at the same time, avoid opportunity losses, the consultant's job is to manage their investment at a steady state. Idle funds are lost opportunities.

Consultants who can offer only sporadic projects, either on their own initiative or in reaction to requests for proposal, are poverty stricken as growers of their clients. Growth that is slowed by excessive meantimes between projects is impoverished growth that will never give its client a consistent competitive advantage. Nor will it provide its consultative project manager with predictable profitability.

The cost-effectiveness of the client-consultant relationship is enhanced by continuity. Conversely, discontinuity enhances only start-up and wind-down costs. Consulting-by-engagements dilutes the consultant's ability to discover networked interrelationships between client operations, interdependencies among processes, and interactions between their critical success factors that can lead to endlessly expansive opportunities to add value.

If he or she is a bona fide partner to a client, a consultant's natural habitat is in residence at his client organization, embedded in the flow of client work, information, and funds. His client partners have easy access to him there, up or down the hall. He has easy access to their problems and opportunities as they arise, on a real-time basis, that precludes their discovery, let alone proposal, by his competitors. The consultant who controls client knowledge controls the account. For all intents and purposes, he functions as an insider. His

preemptive knowledge gives him a perpetual supply of problems and opportunities just as it gives his client partners the
confidence to let him manage the improvement of their
contributions.

Outsiders start from scratch if they try to departner a
resident consultant. If they propose to do merely as well, they
declare themselves to be unnecessary. If they propose to do
better, they are suspect because they do not know what the
resident consultant knows. Nor are they known to his client
partners. They are put in an impossible bind. The more
conservatively they present themselves, the more irrelevant
they appear. Yet the more venturesome their proposals, the
more incredible they make themselves out to be.

4

How to Plan
Service Sales

When you plan to give definition to the type of service you want your business to be, it will help to keep three guidelines in mind:

1. Your service must be a grower of clients in specific industries.
2. Your service must be a grower of specific lines of business (LOBs) and business functions for clients in these industries.
3. Your service must be a grower of specific managers within these business lines and business functions—each client's profit center managers who contribute the major flows of profitable sales volume along with the cost center managers who contribute the major costs. If your service is going to grow them, it must expand and speed up their sales and reduce and slow down their costs.

You may speak of the industries you serve—that is, grow—as your client industries. You may speak of the companies you serve as your client companies. But your only true clients are their managers. Their companies will grow only if you help their managers grow the contributions they make to company profits. This is why service businesses are called personal service businesses: The way to grow a client is

73

through your key people growing its key people. Each of them must be grown personally if you are going to serve them.

Each manager you serve will have his or her own personal business objectives to be a growth contributor. Your role is to accelerate their realization. The first step you must take is to find out what they are.

If you are going to serve a profit-responsible manager of a line of business, you will need to know where his "growth handles" are. Is he being charged with increasing annual inventory turns or reducing the time-to-market of new products or fulfilling orders faster? If you are going to serve a cost-accountable manager of a business function, is he under the gun to reduce design cycle time or the costs of repairs under warranty? The only way to grow a client manager is to grasp his growth handles in a hands-on manner and focus with him on one of his objectives. This makes growth finite, not vaporous, and brings down to earth the otherwise flowery protestations of amateur growers who suck in their cheeks and dedicate themselves holistically to "growing businesses." Managers grow businesses; growers serve by growing business managers.

Growth handles are always highly specific. For this reason, providers of growth services become narrowly focused squinters who look for one handle at a time. When they find it, they grab on to it and never let it go until it is no longer cost-effective to try to improve its contribution. That occurs when the point of diminishing returns is reached, which means that each dollar being invested in growing a manager's contribution begins to yield progressively less return. At that point, new dollars can make more money by being invested somewhere else. This is what asset management is all about.

In order to make sure that you are always operating at your maximum cost-effectiveness as a growth provider, you must maintain a compulsive focus on profit contribution— your own and that of the client managers you partner with.

This means that every grasp of a growth handle must be managed as a profit-improvement project. It must be planned, worked according to its plan, and measured and monitored at each milestone stage of its progress. There will always be three things for you to measure:

1. Each of your partner's improvement in the percentage of profits being made on sales
2. Each of your partner's improved percentage of investment turnover
3. If a partner manages a cost center or a not-for-profit operation, his improved percentage of assets retrieved from operations as a result of reduced or eliminated costs

Planning the Way Your Clients Plan

Objectives are a plan's outcomes. As a service business, you must have two sets of outcomes. First, your clients are grown. Then you must derive your own growth from the growth of your clients. Each of the client-specific plan's objectives answers the question, Where are you taking the client? They answer it by specifying, "To this much added growth."

Strategies are the transitory steps you and your clients must take together to achieve your mutually improved outcomes. While a plan's objectives answer the first question, Where are you taking the client? your strategies answer the next question, How are you going to get there in the most cost-effective manner?

Clients run their businesses on the basis of financial objectives. Sales objectives contribute to them. So do objectives to reduce the costs of doing business. As a result, client strategies are also categorized in these two ways. Some strategies are designed to expand sales revenues or earnings. Other strategies are designed to reduce or eliminate costs. Your objectives and strategies must parallel the way your clients plan if your plans are going to be incremental—that is, additive of values—to their own. Incremental plans are the only kind that can be partnered.

In accounting terms, the profits of a business are said to be its residue. They are the residual gains that are left over after the costs incurred to generate them are paid back. If you are going to be a grower of client businesses, you must think in management terms. You must begin your planning by starting with client profits as the up-front objectives of everything you will do together. A client's incremental profits, which is the portion of his total profits that you will be responsible for, are what you must begin with, not simply end up with.

When your clients start their business plans with profit objectives, they regard profits as the return they receive from their investments to earn them. Their formula for calculating return on investment looks like this:

$$\frac{\text{Net operating profit}}{\text{Total funds invested}} = \text{ROI}$$

According to this formula, managers of the client companies you will plan to grow will already be trying to grow their businesses by using one or both of the following two strategies:

1. They will be trying to increase their net operating profits by turning over sales faster or at higher margins.
2. They will be trying to reduce their total funds invested to achieve the same net operating profits or increased profits.

These bedrock client strategies must become your strategies. If a client is planning to turn over his sales faster, you must help him. If he is planning to turn them over at higher margins, you must help him. If he is planning to reduce his costs of turning over his sales, you must help him. Whatever he is planning to do, you must help him do it better, faster, and with greater certainty. If you do these things, you will serve him well.

Just as each client's objectives precondition his strategies, your strategies must be predetermined by your clients' objectives. By serving your clients' objectives, you can ensure that your plan's strategies will be compatible with the mix that each of your clients is already planning. By helping him achieve results that are over and above his forecasts, it will be easy for both of you to measure the incremental values you add and to prove your fit.

Putting Client Objectives First

Services are marketable only if they provide client growth. Service sales plans must therefore be accelerated growth plans. Unless you plan to grow your clients, you will never be able to maximize your sales or to make the most margins from them.

The best way to plan to grow a client is to plan to add the additional value of your growth to his business. A partnered growth plan like this does two things:

1. It makes your client's growth the prime objective of your service.
2. It makes your service a prime strategy for your client's growth.

Planning your sales as a service provider should be done on a client-by-client basis. Each client growth plan should be based on five assessments of "what's in it for both of us":

1. What is this client's most likely growth potential from partnering with me? Growth potential represents your optimal penetration, where his return and yours exceed their investments by acceptable rates of return for both of you.
2. At the most likely growth potential, what are our most likely mutual cash flows over a three-year time frame? Cash flow is the cash proceeds from revenues minus cash outlays.
3. At the most likely annualized cash flows, what are our most likely mutual net profits over the three-year time frame?

4. Over the three-year time frame, when is the most likely onset of parity competition with my product or service technology that can reduce my premium margins to commodity levels or force me to increase my investment to regain primacy? If I increase my investment, what effect will that have on the investment I must require from my client? If I cannot regain primacy cost-effectively, what new service opportunity can I migrate to where I can once again merit prime margins based on client growth potential?

5. If I migrate to an alternative service opportunity within the three-year time frame of my plan, shall I make my own capability, partner it, or buy it? If I partner, with whom? If I buy, from whom?

These assessments make it necessary for you to plan on the basis of putting client objectives first and keeping them foremost throughout the life of your plans. They acknowledge that you are planning client growth; that your own growth will be derived from your client's growth and therefore comes second; that growth is based on improved profits and that improved profits come from improved client cash flows as a result of reduced costs or expanded sales; that services are perishable, subject to replication and commoditization by competition, and therefore they must be continually renewed if they are to keep their margin power.

At each annual planning cycle, you can appraise your client growth plans by making four inquiries of your commitments:

1. Is our service *proprietary* enough? Is it the best match-up we can make between our client's needs and our capabilities? Are these needs the best use of our capabilities? Is this client the best potential benefiter from our capabilities? What other or different capabilities would benefit him more? What other or different client would benefit more from them?

2. Is our positioning *differentiated* enough? Is our service benefit presented in a preemptive enough manner to rule out competitive debate? Is it presented as the industry standard?

3. Are our strategies *minimal* enough? Are we maximizing our mutual growth objectives with the smallest, least expensive asset base? Are we controlling the costs of growth for both of us?

4. Are we *monitoring* our growth early and often enough? Are our measurement milestones front-end loaded in the initial phases of our joint plans to give us early warning of problems while they are readily correctable? Have we identified the earliest checkpoint where we may want to or have to revise our strategy mix? Do we have an inventory of strategies ready to choose from to rejuvenate or restructure our plan?

A Statement of Objective along the lines of the model shown in Figure 4-1 will help keep each of your plans in focus. You can use it to test your strategies as you plan them. Is everything we are planning contributing to the $6 million outcome we have promised our client by year three? Are we doing all the right things to achieve his $2.5 million cost reduction? Is there anything more we should be doing to make sure his earnings on increased sales go up by $3.5 million? Are we doing anything that can be counterproductive?

Figure 4-1. Statement of objective.

Our minimum objective is to increase the contribution to corporate profits made by your process control operations by a total of 30 percent over a three-year cycle, yielding an incremental pretax gain of $6 million by year three. This objective will be met by reducing $2.5 million in cost contributions currently being made by your operations and increasing marketable yield with an earnings contribution at current margins of $3.5 million.

Planning Growth Backwards

Since service businesses are committed to their clients' growth as the precondition to their own growth, their planning process must work backwards in two dimensions:

1. Your growth plans should originate outside your business, in the businesses of your clients. Each of your plans' starting points is where the plans of your clients leave off. In this way, your growth objectives for them will always be incremental to their own growth. By beginning your plans where client plans end, you can be genuinely additive to their competitiveness. This is the meaning of being "customer driven."

2. Your growth plans should be started at the end of your one- to three-year planning horizon and work their way backwards to the present. In this way, you can be certain of "getting there from here" since your plan process starts "there." This will help ensure that you achieve your objectives with the minimal mix of strategies allocated in their optimal sequence.

Backwards planning relieves you of some of the superhuman assumptions that are involved in traditional forecasting. It substitutes aftcasting for forward planning by causing you to look backwards from your objectives to ask the question: *What must have had to have happened* in order for each of our successive planned milestones to have been reached?

Planning backwards *as if* you had already achieved each objective gives you a different perspective on what strategic options are available to you, what you can do with them, and what their most plausible outcomes would probably have been. You will be able to create new and different alternative strategy scenarios, writing them retrospectively to replicate their most likely impacts, so you can see if your forward-looking determinations will be correct about your most critical success factors.

In order to make certain you plan backwards, it is a good idea to set up your plan's profit and revenue objectives according to the model in Figure 4-2 and your own profit and revenue to investment ratios according to the model in Figure 4-3. These models summarize for you the relationship between the profit values you add to a customer and the profit values he adds back to you. They show your yield as a grower and the reward you receive for it.

Figures 4-4 and 4-5 summarize the two sources of your revenues and earnings: The opportunities you capitalize to reduce customer business function costs are shown in Figure 4-4 and your opportunities to help realize increased customer sales are shown in Figure 4-5.

It is important for you to keep in mind that you and each of your clients represent investments that each of you makes in the other. You also represent returns to each other on these investments. Your mutual returns are the reasons you do business together. As a service provider, you will have to learn to think of yourself as an investment manager for your

Figure 4-2. Profit/revenue objectives.

	Year 1 (19XX) ($000)	Year 2 (19XX) ($000)	Year 3 (19XX) ($000)
Profit Objectives to Client (profit contributed to Client by us)			
Profit Objectives to Us (profit contributed to us by Client)			
Revenue Objectives to Client (revenue contributed to Client by us)			
Revenue Objectives to Us (revenue contributed to us by Client)			

Figure 4-3. Profit/revenue-to-investment ratios.

	Year 1 (19XX)	Year 2 (19XX)
Profit-Investment Ratio	__ : __	__ : __
	($000)	($000)
Incremental Profit	_____	_____
Incremental Investment	_____	_____
Revenue-Investment Ratio	__ : __	__ : __
	($000)	($000)
Incremental Revenue	_____	_____
Incremental Investment	_____	_____

Figure 4-4. Customer cost-reduction opportunities.

	Business Function		
Cost Problems	Value of Cost Problem ($000)	Value From Our Solution ($000)	Investment for Our Solution ($000)
1. _____	$ _____	$ _____	$ _____
2. _____	_____	_____	_____
3. _____	_____	_____	_____
4. _____	_____	_____	_____
5. _____	_____	_____	_____

Figure 4-5. Customer sales expansion opportunities.

Sales Opportunities	*Line of Business*		
	Value of Opportunity ($000)	*Value From Our Solution ($000)*	*Investment for Our Solution ($000)*
1. _____	$ _____	$ _____	$ _____
2. _____	_____	_____	_____
3. _____	_____	_____	_____
4. _____	_____	_____	_____
5. _____	_____	_____	_____

clients' assets, a grower of your clients' funds. Clients will judge your skills at managing their money by the returns you are able to make for them: how many more dollars they get back on every dollar they invest with you, how quickly they get back their principal sums and how fast the earnings on them accrue, and how predictable you are as a reliable money-maker.

Getting Your Priorities Right

Three planning strategies form the tripod that must platform your start-up growth base: an *industry-specific* position as a grower, a *function-specific* concentration on where you grow clients best, and a *results-specific* emphasis on client profit-improvement.

A single business purpose. In order to possess commercial integrity, your transformed service business must profess a single purpose that preselects your clients. Your business must be immediately discernible by them as "the one that grows my type of business best."

A single business market. You must concentrate on growing a single business line or business function in a single industry as your client base and become its functional and industry standards of added value.

A single business objective. Profit improvement of your clients must be your single objective for being in business. All your other objectives must be subordinate to it.

A business growth plan is the proper place for getting these three priorities straight. Guiding your sales plans with them will require you to manage the return you make on the investment of your assets in client growth. You will know when you are managing professionally when your rate of return cannot be improved any further without adding to or subtracting from your investment. That means you are getting every last bit of mileage out of your current asset base.

Your prime priority should be to invest in achieving a preemptive position as the industry standard for growing the client operations you select to grow. This position, sometimes called your image, will turn out to be your most precious asset. It must say three things for you:

1. We grow these lines of business or business functions in your industry best. Nobody does it better.
2. Our standards are the ones to beat. They are the standards of the most cost-effective competitive advantage.
3. If your standards already equal ours, we can help you maintain them. If they do not equal ours, we can bring you closer to them.

A position that says these three things about you will rule out client debates on your merits versus the merits of competitive suppliers. They will all have to beat you or you will win by default. This will make them reactive to your standards; you will be the standard-bearer and they will be reduced to being also-ran commodity suppliers who, as equals to each other, will be able to sell only at commodity margins.

The preemptiveness of your position will be a function of two assets. The first is how much you know and how well you know it about the current cost clusters and latent revenue opportunities in the client processes where you specialize. This database will comprise your growth engine. The second asset is how well your people can apply your service solutions—their expertise in application, installation, implementation, information, education, and consultation. They will be the drivers of your growth engine.

Testing Negative for Philanthropy

Finding client managers that you can grow is the genesis of a business-to-business service. There are two types of managers to look for:

1. Who is agonized by costs he does not want or need and cannot afford that are the type I am good at helping to reduce?
2. Who is tantalized by revenues he wants and needs but cannot realize that are the type I am good at helping to bring in?

This is your service market: the agonized and the tantalized. The first suffers from excessive direct costs. The second suffers from excessive opportunity costs. If you could put one word into the mouths of either of them, it would say "Help!"

If you identify yourself as a help provider, you must be sure that the help you can provide is a paying proposition for both you and your clients. Two criteria must be met before your help can pay for itself:

1. A client's prospective profits from your help should exceed his current direct costs or opportunity costs.
2. A client's prospective profits from your help should exceed his investment with you to obtain the profits. In turn, your own profits from helping the client

should exceed your direct costs to provide help or your opportunity costs from not providing it to an even more profitable client.

When these two sets of conditions are met, everybody wins. This is the scenario for saying yes to service. The contrary scenario for saying no is when only you or your clients can win. This will happen when a client's investment with you exceeds his prospective profits from your help or when your costs to provide help exceed your own prospective profits in return. Each of these propositions is self-defeating because it is cost-ineffective. If you turn out to be a provider of negative growth—if your clients consistently get back less than a dollar for each dollar they invest in you—you will become their long-term terminator. If you grow clients who are unable to grow you back, you will turn out to be a short-term philanthropist.

In order to be sure that you consistently test negative for philanthropy, you must temper service with cost-effectiveness. It is never sufficient to ask, Can I help? The word *cost-effectively* must be appended to each question. Can I help? is meaningless as a business question without qualifying it with, Does it pay? and quantifying it with, How much does it pay and how soon?

Even caring-type services whose mission is "quality care" cannot neglect the cost-effectiveness of providing it if they are being managed as profit-making businesses. Unless a provider is profitable, the only quality of care that can be provided will be low. If you provide low-quality care, your business partners will be deprived of their optimal growth; you will be suboptimizing your service to them. The less you are able to grow them, the less they will be able to grow you back in return. If you are both lucky, mutual *slowth*—continued slow growth—is the worst case you will have to deal with. More likely, you will find yourselves winding down together.

5

How to Choose From the Three Basic Service Models

When it comes to choosing your type of service business, there are three basic models:

1. *Systems integration.* You can make a client's operation work better because you integrate its component parts more cost-effectively.
2. *Process reengineering.* You can make a client's operation work better because you restructure, resize, redesign, and reengineer its process to run faster or more productively or less expensively.
3. *Facility/category management.* You can make a client's operation work better because you manage or comanage it to reduce its costs or increase its revenues so that it adds more to his profits or adds them more quickly or more reliably.

These three models represent ascending levels of implementation by a supplier in a client's business. At the systems integration level, the supplier coordinates a client's assets to make a function work better that may already be working well. At the process reengineering level, the supplier rearranges, renovates, or replaces client assets that are obsolete or obsolescent. At the facility or category management level, a client's operation may remain internal but it becomes managed by a supplier, or it is outsourced to the supplier to be run off premises and off the books.

For your first transformation of a product-based business to a service, you should choose the model that represents the minimal solution to a client's problem or opportunity. The "rule of the minimal solution" will help you ensure the cost-effectiveness of your service, minimize client disruption, and keep you from biting off more than you can chew.

You will need four assets in your start-up transformation kit:

1. You must have a database that identifies the process flow of the client business function that you are going to integrate, reengineer, or manage so that you can calculate its critical cost problems and critical revenue opportunities.

2. You must have a cost-effective solution to one or more of the critical cost problems and critical revenue opportunities whose contribution to client profit improvement you can quantify in both dollar and time values.

3. You must have a consultative manager who can plan, implement, and measure the value of your solution in a joint working environment where client satisfaction will be maximized. The manager must have access to a multifunctional team of technical, financial, and information resources who can partner with their client correlates.

4. You must have a compelling proposition to persuade a client to go ahead with you. Your proposition must answer questions like these:

- Why this particular solution?
- Why this size investment?
- Why this length of payback?
- Why this consultant?
- Why not do something else with someone else?
- Why not do nothing?

If you are a small company, you may ask how you can play the game in competition with megacorp integrators, reengineers, and facility managers who have access to superior assets. You can play and win if you can answer *yes* to any one of three questions:

1. Do you have an innovative way to apply a technology? Your technology can be a science or it can be in sales, distribution, or marketing. Your capability should be in the basic applications skills of installing, implementing, and integrating a customer's use of the technology in order to maximize its cost-effectiveness.

2. Do you have specialized knowledge of a market niche? Your knowledge should be in the areas of its business needs for growth, the business problems that are constraining the realization of its growth needs, and the business solutions that can correct them in the most cost-effective manner.

3. Do you have proprietary training and development skills? Your skills should enable you to train a customer's managers to apply profit-improvement operating strategies whose results will pay back the investment to train them.

Model One: Systems Integration
and
Model Two: Process Reengineering

During the 1980s, the core operations in virtually every industry began to come under critical review. Most of them had been going on unchanged in any basic way since the 1950s, making them overdue for significant alteration. In the course of their heyday of a quarter of a century or more, the cost structures of many processes had shifted from a concentration on production, particularly labor and materials, to the costs of information accessing and integration. Productivity standards had changed along with them. So had every industry's definition of quality. Zero defects and zero inventory strategies were changing the face of office and factory work.

Operating just in time was in; operating fat, just in case, was out. Hierarchies of management structures or, for that matter, redundant resources of any kind, were no longer tolerable. Waste in the form of scrap, downtime, or prolonged cycle times was unaffordable. If you were inefficient, you were going to have to pay for it one way or another. Whether it cost you capital or market share was up to you.

As a result, the Kaizen strategy of continuous system and process improvement has become a necessity. Change is no longer a once-every-generation event; it takes place whenever a significant competitive advantage can be gained, however transient it may be. People and their processes are now flexed over and over again to do things differently and to do different things. Innovative ways of organizing and operating businesses result in the formation of "adhocracies" that cut through the layers of internal hierarchies or do away with them. They bring suppliers and customers into planning, development, and implementation operations as full-fledged partners so that total quality specifications can be engineered into every transaction from the start. They make suppliers into joint venturers and cooperators of their customers' processes.

There is still a long way to go. By some accounts, manufacturing businesses have only been able to improve their average productivity by less than 1 percent a year over twenty-five years while service businesses have hardly improved at all.

Every organization scheme and operational process in every business is in play. In an attempt to answer "Where's the beef?" their sacred cows are being ground into hamburger:

- Whenever a significant cost exists that can be shown to be unnecessary, there is a universally implicit invitation—indeed, a demand—to fix it.
- Whenever a significant amount of money is being left on the table as a result of opportunity costs from unrealized sales or by pricing schedules that are trading away margins for the sake of volume, there is a universally implicit demand to bring in the money.

Since many inefficient or obsolescent systems are incapable of significantly reducing the costs they contribute or expanding their sales no matter how well they are managed, they need to be reintegrated, restructured, revised, and reengineered.

They need to be rightsized, realigned, and rationalized to align them with the stringent new cost and profit requirements imposed by global competition and to enable them to make a faster, larger, and more consistent contribution to competitiveness. Renovation, innovation, or obliteration is the order of the day, not simply for the way in which processes are operated but for the conceptual foundations of entire processes themselves.

Process revision takes two main forms along a continuum. One is systems integration, the *realignment* of an operation. The other is process reengineering, the *redesign* of an operation, from end to end if necessary, to improve its contributions to quality and productivity.

Systems integration and process reengineering are Mutt and Jeff services. Their sequencing can go either way. A system can be integrated or reintegrated therapeutically so that the process it controls does not have to be reengineered. This says that the process is structurally sound but its operations are suboptimizing its performance. Or a system can be integrated remedially after a process has been taken apart and put back together in a new way.

Integrating or Being Integrated

Your current customers ceaselessly search for the optimal mix of ingredients and components for their operating processes. If they ever seize it, it is only for a fleeting moment since optimization always carries with it the qualification "for this time."

An optimal mix is a minimal mix that is organized for maximum cost-effectiveness. Mix management is an integrating service that coordinates the discreet parts of a process to ensure their efficient interaction. As customer mixes become more technologically sophisticated and driven by information sciences, the need to ensure their harmonious networking becomes imperative. Automation creates and enhances efficiencies. By the same token, it magnifies inefficiencies.

Your customers have three choices for optimizing their systems. One is to do it themselves. Another is to do it with you. A third is to do it with one of your competitors.

If a competitor integrates one of the customer systems that you presently sell into, your products and product-related services may become integrated into his systems. He will come between you and your customer—in effect, he will become your customer. You will be unable to sell through him or around him to your end users; you will have to sell to him, under his terms and conditions. He will deal with you as a vendor, issuing straitjacketed requests for proposal like the example shown in Figure 5-1 that will lock you into the position of a product-based subcontractor.

Not only will your margins be shut down. You will be shut out of access to your former customer decision-makers and the access to customer business plans that goes with it. You will have been downgraded to a tier two business, a supplier's supplier, who is able to do business only at the pleasure of your tier one competitors. They will capture the role of your customers' consultants. Any hope you may have of converting your customers into clients will disappear.

Because the penalties are so competitively disadvantageous, the rule you must observe is to *integrate or be integrated.*

Figure 5-1. Integrator request for proposal.

"Design a brake set that will stop a 2,200-pound car within 200 feet at 60 miles an hour, and that can perform a minimum of 10 times in succession without fading more than 10 percent between the first and tenth application. The brake set must fit within a 12-inch housing and weigh a maximum of 2 pounds. The original price must not exceed $40 a set and must be progressively reduced each year by 3 to 7 percent."

In a business environment where there is no middle ground, you can either lead your customers to optimize their functional mixes or stand by and have your business led by someone who will.

If you miss out becoming an integrator and end up being integrated, you will have to learn how to keep every one of your costs down, how to perfect every just-in-time practice, and how to assure quality at a zero defect level of performance in every operation. Otherwise you will never be able to make it as the lowest margin, highest quality bidder. As you and other integrateds are brought together under the leadership of your customers' integrators, your industry will come to resemble a Japanese Kieretsu, a loose grouping of independent businesses into a family relationship of convenience.

In the 1990s, it will be a rare company that will not belong to several integrator teams. Many of these relationships will be virtually permanent as the same suppliers get good at partnering with each other under the same prime contractors. Other relationships will be periodic, on an as-needed basis, with each integrator choosing up sides against competitive integrators. For these companies, their prime contractor's caveat "Integrate or be integrated" will be adapted for them to read "Be integrated or obliterated."

Optimizing a Customer's Mix

A systems integrator is a major domo supplier who acts as a single point of contact with his client to plan, design, and manage the implementation of a comprehensive business solution for a client's operating process. He acts like a choreographer, orchestrating the assembly and implementation of a network of multivendor products and product-related services. If he is a manufacturer, his own products may or may not be included. More important than products are two skillsets. One is the ability to manage large-scale profit-improvement projects. The other is the ability to manage multiple-partner business alliances.

Each alliance brings to the integrator's optimal mix a product or product-related service that he has selected because it fits best into the system he is integrating. In this way, each system is "vertical": customized to be specific to its function and to the integrator's client so that it will be sure to yield the proposed amount of new profits that the integrator has sold and his client has bought off on.

A systems integrator must work on two levels, macro and micro. On the macro level, he must develop and implement his solutions to serve each client's vision of his business, his strategies for achieving it, and the availability of his funds. Then on a micro level, the integrator must be a professional project manager with high-level problem-solving and communications skills, good estimating, purchasing, and pricing skills, and the ability to analyze risk. This duality of working levels requires the best people. In systems integration, there are no hardware or software solutions. Solutions are business-improvement solutions that lower customer costs and expand customer revenues and earnings. These are primarily people skills. They deal only secondarily with product proficiency.

The best-skilled people have a combination of industry and operating experience in the business functions that you are going to integrate. They will be natural mentors of operating people so that they can empower their clients to manage their newly integrated systems. And they will be partnerable so that they can inspire trust.

Proposing an Integrated System

A customer you are supplying today will permit you to manage the integration of one of his systems if you can prove that the initial cost of the integrated system will quickly be paid back by its improved cash flows and that its life-cycle costs will be self-capitalizing from subsequent cash flows. These results will prove that his system is "running better" as a result of your integration and, as a consequence, so is his business.

In order to be able to propose improved profit contributions from integrating a customer system, you will need to own or be able to lease or buy your own integrated system of resources that range from pedestrian to exotic. For example,

- You will need resources to track competitive technologies and their suppliers so that you have a knowledge pool of tier two vendors to integrate.
- You will need resources to generate profit-improvement proposals that deliver superior cost-effective solutions.
- You will need resources to balance the customer's need to maintain a stable operating environment with the ability to technically upgrade each system on a progressive, incremental schedule.

Your resources will have to be flexible enough to work in partnership with multifunction multivendor teams. No two integrations are likely to be replicas. Each operation, even if it is a similar process in the same industry, almost always turns out to be unique. Your alliances will be different too, combining partners on a deal-by-deal basis whose capabilities will be specific to each project's needs.

A proposal to integrate a customer's system must be presented as a business proposition before the customer can be converted to a client. As a business case, it must set financial and operational objectives, define the critical success factors that will determine realization of the objectives, and prescribe the single best solution that will affect the critical factors most cost-effectively. The solution's technology will come second. Your proposal agenda will look like this:

- *Set objectives.* Calculate revised bottom-line contributions that the integrated system will make to customer competitiveness in terms of:
  1. Financial performance contributions to costs and revenues
  2. Operational performance contributions to quality, productivity, and customer satisfaction that will yield the financial contributions

• *Identify critical success factors.* Define the minimum re-configurations of operational work flows whose integration or reintegration will account for the maximum amount of improved contribution in the minimum amount of time at minimum investment by outlining:

1. The best place to start to maximize short-term results without compromising long-term success
2. A step-by-step migration plan from one successfully achieved objective to another

• *Design the single best solution.* Develop the one best solution that is most likely to achieve the objectives of the integrated system by acknowledging the solution's critical success factors in three models:

1. A model of the single-source management team that will implement the single best solution and achieve its objectives according to the planned financial and operational models the team will manage
2. A financial pro forma model to prototype the economic contributions from system integration, showing a before-and-after cost-benefit analysis of the annual cash flows derived from cost reduction or revenue expansion along the lines of Figure 5-2
3. An operational model to prototype the functional contributions from system integration, showing a before-and-after performance analysis of the annual improvements in quality, productivity, and customer satisfaction that will contribute to the financial model

Reengineering Operating Processes

When a customer process gets reengineered, it can undergo a single operational improvement or a reconstruction of its entire work flow in which people and their outputs get a thorough going-over. The reengineer's scrutiny ranges from a relatively innocent inquiry such as "Does it have to be done like this?" to a greater order of magnitude that asks "Does it have to be done at all?"

Figure 5-2. Cost-benefit analysis.

	Year 0	Year 1	Year 2
1. New equipment investment			
2. Revenue			
3. Cash savings			
4. Noncash expense			
5. Depreciation ACRS			
6. Material trade-in			
7. Profit improvements BIT (3 – 5 + 6)			
8. LESS: income tax (%)			
9. Investment tax credit (10%)			
10. NET PROFIT IMPROVEMENT (7 – 8 + 9)			

11. CASH FLOW (1 + 5 + 10)			
12. PAYBACK (cumulative cash flow)			
13. Present value (10% factor)			
14. Discounted cash flow (11 × 13)			
15. NET PRESENT VALUE CASH FLOW (14)			
16. RETURN ON INVESTMENT (10 ÷ 1)			

FIGURE 5-2   SAME SIZE   **PROFITS WITHOUT PRODUCTS**

The three criteria that exert the greatest influence on the answers are cost-benefits, productivity, and quality. They are amplified by evaluations of meantimes, downtimes, cycle times, and lead times; flexibility of current systems to respond to market-driven needs, just-in-time efficiencies; elimination of wasteful duplication and nonproductive redundancies; and measurements of customer satisfaction.

Reengineering takes new approaches to traditionally run processes and modernizes current processes to bring them up to state-of-the-art. Any cost center and revenue or profit center is fair game, whether it is concerned with factory-type operations such as manufacturing or office-type operations such as planning, administration, or sales. In the course of reengineering, the mission of a process as well as its organization and operations can come in for redefinition.

Many managers have stopped being "open to buy" to their regular suppliers because they want to avoid what they call "paving the cowpaths"—adding more costs to an already faulty or obsolete process that incurs a risk of nullifying any beneficial impacts from new equipment. Instead, they are being challenged by process reengineers to go back to the drawing board and answer questions like these:

- Has every major reducible cost been reduced?
- Has every noncontributing operation been divested?
- Has every labor-intensive task been automated?

The emergence of process reengineering as a major service business opportunity is an admission that the traditional method of calling in reactive expediters on a crisis basis has become obsolete. Today's premium is on preventing a crisis, not resolving it. This can be accomplished only by embracing continuous improvement. Instead of inspecting for quality at certain key points in a process and undertaking rework when it is not there, managers must reengineer their processes so that quality is built in at each step of the way. Instead of measuring only the inputs of resources that go into their processes, managers must also measure their outputs in terms of repairs under warranty, recalls, value-based margins, and customer satisfaction.

Reengineering may sound like it applies only to a customer's manufacturing processes. A better name would be "process remodeling" since it involves the substitution of a new, improved model of the way a business function is operated for the model that is currently in place. Remodeling can apply to any process, including the everyday office processes of decision making and decision support, strategic business development, and project funding. The same ground rules apply. You must be a minimalist, helping your customer managers to organize each process into the smallest work unit possible and staff the smallest number of workers who operate on a just-in-time basis. Each worker should be trained to be multifunctional. Each work unit should be an autonomous cost or profit center so that its contribution can be measured and its workers rewarded according to their contributions.

In order to become a reengineer, you will need three sets of customer data:

1. How a customer's process currently flows, mapped from start to finish as in Figure 5-3
2. Where its major costs cluster and how much each cluster contributes to negative cash flows
3. Where its major revenue sources cluster and how much each cluster contributes to positive cash flows

Exercising Reengineering Muscles

Developing an eye for reengineering opportunities and focusing your thinking on how to seize them takes practice in the exercise of your "if-then" muscles:

"*If* we knew that a customer was having this kind of cost problem in a production process in his business that we sell into, *then* we could convert him to a client by restructuring the way his process works in these key cost-producing areas and come up with this improved result within this period of time."

Figure 5-3. Aerospace manufacturing process flow.

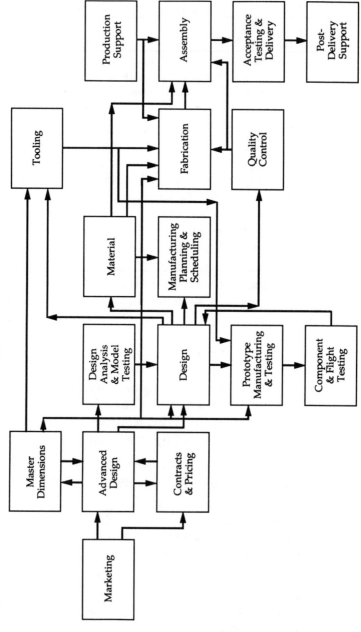

"If we knew that a customer was having this kind of revenue problem in a sales or marketing process in his business that we sell into, *then* we could convert him to a client by restructuring the way his process works in these key revenue-producing areas and come up with this improved result within this period of time."

Putting yourself into other people's businesses outside your own industry on an as-if basis—as if you did what each of them does and you wanted to transform their product-based business to a reengineering service—can help give you additional practice in acquiring a service mindset:

• Suppose you are a product-based business that sells computer systems to automate the accounts payable functions of multisupplier manufacturing companies like Ford Motor Company and you want to segue into a process reengineering service. Your first step is to rethink Ford's current system for paying its bills and then redesign the process wherever re-engineering can be cost-effective anywhere along the work flow of the process from placing the order to paying the bill.

You will have to know Ford's *"before* process" with its current flows, productivity, and contributions to time and dollar costs. Then you will have to envision the optimal *"after* process" after you have reengineered it. How much will work flow have to be speeded to take advantage of thirty-day discounts? How much money will be saved? How many fewer people and how many computers will be required and how will they be integrated? How much more productive will they be?

If Ford's *before* process employs 500 people, whereas competitor Mazda employs only five, what is the most likely headcount you can predict for Ford's *after* process? If Ford's *before* process requires information to be matched a total of fourteen times as one department after another hands off each payable to the next one, whereas competitor Honda needs only four transactions, what is the most likely number of data-matching transactions you can predict for Ford's *after* process? How much will your reengineered process contribute to Ford's competitive advantage if its turnaround time can be reduced two-thirds by being driven from payments on receipt of goods instead of receipt of invoice?

• Suppose you sell your computer systems to the policy underwriting functions of insurance companies like Aetna and you want to segue into a process reengineering service. Your first step is to rethink Aetna's current system for underwriting policies and then redesign the process wherever reengineering can be cost-effective.

You will have to know Aetna's *before* process of issuing a policy, how much time and dollar cost is added at each step, and how much money is being lost because Aetna cannot bill its customers until a policy is sent out. Then you will have to envision the optimal *after* process when each policy can be issued faster.

If Aetna's *before* process takes thirty steps spanning five departments and occupying time from nineteen people to issue a policy, what is the most likely result of eliminating all work handoffs from one desk to another in Aetna's *after* process? How much improved profit would Aetna's policy underwriting function be able to contribute if its lead time were condensed from an average of fifteen days to 3.5 days, getting each policy out in a quarter of an hour instead of four hours?

Instead of serving Aetna's policy underwriting operations, you could be in a business of reengineering the cost-effectiveness of its claims handling process. Instead of serving only Aetna, you could similarly reengineer the same processes in other insurance companies; instead of only reengineering insurance companies, you could broaden your market in the financial services industry to include reducing the costs, speeding the productivity, and increasing the resulting revenues from reengineering the mortgage business functions of banks. By selling a process reengineering service that allowed twenty or so people to convene electronically to work on all aspects of each mortgage application at once, you could attach your price to the added value of your service and simply bundle your computer systems into it without ever having to sell them.

Reengineering Organization Processes

Organization structures are being reengineered across all industries so that "less manages more." Fewer top managers manage. More of their mid-level managers are being empowered with autonomy and, in turn, are charged with making a contribution to profits. Fewer internal services support each manager. Fewer decisions are handed down to them from above, and access to information rather than access to senior management executives has become the great conveyor of power.

If your product-based business sells into the management processes of your customer hierarchies, you can help them reengineer their organization structure and its work flows along the lines of newly emergent models like the Flat Top and the Spider Web.

• *The Flat Top.* The stereotypical organization pyramid is being reengineered into the Flat Top model shown in Figure 5-4. The Flat Top is a vertical, top-down model that is marked by three changes:

1. A minimal team of strategic business-unit (SBU) managers plans objectives for a process and allocates funds to resource it against the plan's objectives.
2. A minimal team of professional business managers runs the process with help from a minimal internal support staff and outside consultants.
3. A minimal team of process operators staffs the process, supported by automation and the guidelines of their industry's best practices.

• *The Spider Web.* The Spider Web (shown in Figure 5-5) is a business network model that has decentralized the ways that power, information distribution, and control can flow. A central management team sits at the web's focal point and acts

Figure 5-4. Flat Top/Pyramid models.

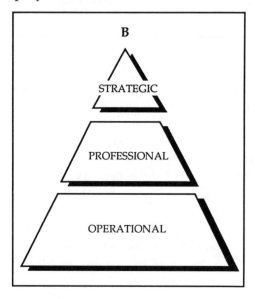

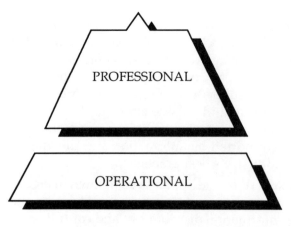

FIGURE 5-4   SAME SIZE   PROFITS WITHOUT PRODUCTS

Figure 5-5. The Spider Web model.

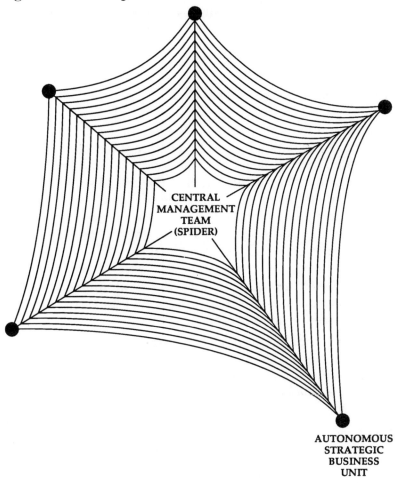

CENTRAL
MANAGEMENT
TEAM
(SPIDER)

AUTONOMOUS
STRATEGIC
BUSINESS
UNIT

as the spider in its control of objectives, funds to be allocated, and stewardship of the business vision. Webbing outward from the center are autonomous business units that are connected to the center and to each other by information technology. Each strategic business unit in the net is a profit center with its own internal and external sources of supply.

Instead of being centered on its product or services in the manner of a traditional business department or division, each profit-centered SBU is centered on a vertically niched market. This salutes its customers, not its products, as the sources of its growth.

Proposing a Reengineering

A proposal to reengineer a customer's process must be presented as a business proposition before the customer can be converted to a client. As a business case, it must set financial and operational objectives, define the critical success factors that will determine realization of the objectives, and prescribe the single best solution that will affect the critical factors most cost-effectively. The solution's technology will come second. Your proposal agenda will look like this:

• *Set objectives.* Calculate revised bottom-line contributions that the reengineered process will make to customer competitiveness in terms of:

1. Financial performance contributions to costs and revenues.
2. Operational performance contributions to quality, productivity, and customer satisfaction that will yield the financial contributions.

• *Identify critical success factors.* Define the minimum number of functions whose renovation or restructuring will account for the maximum amount of improved contribution in the minimum amount of time at minimum investment by outlining:

1. The best place to start to maximize short-term results without compromising long-term success.
2. A step-by-step migration plan from one successfully achieved objective to another.

• *Design the single best solution.* Develop the one best solution that is most likely to achieve the objectives of the reengineered process by acknowledging the solution's critical success factors in three models.

1. A model of the single-source management team that will implement the single best solution and achieve its objectives according to the planned financial and operational models the team will manage.
2. A financial pro-forma model to prototype the economic contributions from reengineering, showing a before-and-after cost-benefit analysis of the annual cash flows derived from cost reduction or revenue expansion along the lines of Figure 5-2.
3. An operational model to prototype the functional contributions from reengineering, showing a before-and-after performance analysis of the annual improvements in quality, productivity, and customer satisfaction that will contribute to the financial model.

Managing Integration and Reengineering Projects

Project management skills are necessary capabilities to be successful in systems integration and processing reengineering. Each integration of a system or restructuring of a process is a business project. As such, you must manage it like a new business venture, complete with its own project plan, profit contribution analysis, and critical path from start to completion.

Every business project starts out as an attempt to make a predicted improvement in a current cost situation or revenue flow. Its objectives are expressed in terms of *expected value* (EV). The project manager's EV is a resolution of two factors:

1. The most likely impact, called the *payoff*.
2. The most likely probability of the predicted payoff being delivered on time within the predicted cost, called the *risk*. A project qualifies as a "go" when its payoff exceeds its risk.

Two sets of criteria, financial and operational, govern the preferred rank order of selection of integration and reengineering projects:

• *Financial criteria.* Projects must meet your respective client's hurdle rate for minimum added value. Projects with the best added value beyond the hurdle rate become preferred investments.

The added value proposed by a project permits it to be directly compared with a customer's other options for investing his funds on the basis of commonly held criteria: After all outlays for investment have been subtracted and the time value of the money to be invested has been factored in, how much return will we get back on our investment from reduced costs and increased revenues and how soon will we get it?

Three financial criteria are always applied to a potential project:

1. How do the annual cash flows accumulate on a year-to-year basis over the commercial life of the project? At what rate? For how long?
2. When does payback of the initial investment occur so that the project's investment can be recovered and recycled, removing the project from risk and allowing it to become self-capitalizing?
3. How much proceeds does the project develop for each dollar laid out? What rate of interest on our money does that represent?

The rate of return on the resources to be invested in a project you propose is one decision-making standard. Another is its opposite: the opportunity cost of not going ahead with a project. What added value will be given up? What competitive advantage will be lost or handed over? What kind of position will that leave us in for the next cycling of our operation?

• *Operational criteria.* Projects must make the minimum disruptive impact on operations required to maximize their financial condition. Projects with the best contributions to improved productivity and quality that incur the lowest costs of retooling, restructuring, and retraining become preferred investments.

In order to improve productivity, a project must reduce the costs of output or increase the quantity and quality of marketable products that a process generates. Costs of output are typically reduced by replacing labor content with automation or cutting down on materials and energy intensity. Quality can be enhanced by reducing product defects and improving product "fit and finish."

You will find that the best project managers run to type. Their type is Type A, which means they are most likely to share characteristics in common like these:

— Personally identify with their projects as "mine"
— One-shot summary decision making
— Bias for completion
— Distaste for ambiguity
— Compulsively time-driven and deadline-oriented
— Multiphasic ability to do several tasks at once
— Let nothing get in the way of success

Model Three: Facility/Category Management

Through the middle of the 1980s, it was standard operating procedure for most companies to do everything in-house. In their telecommunications and computer functions, for example, senior managers believed in running corporate networks themselves with their own equipment and people. As the cost-effectiveness of their ownership became increasingly questionable, many managers began to view the information technologies (IT) of telecommunications and data processing as peripheral to the businesses they were in and saw value in reallocating IT resources to concentrate on their core strategic operations.

As a result, companies began to turn to outsourced suppliers to run their telecommunications and computer networks. One of the first, Eastman Kodak Company, has retained IBM to manage its worldwide data communications facilities and, at the same time, has invested $40 million to retain Digital Equipment Corporation to manage its telecommunications operations. In their roles as facility managers with Kodak, IBM and DEC have transformed their former equipment-based businesses with Kodak into a management service. The chief deliverable of the service is freed-up money for Kodak from cost savings along with new revenues from the sale of freed-up capacity.

Following the Kodak models, telecommunications carriers are increasingly becoming outsourcers of corporate networks. AT&T and the North American business unit of British Telecommunications jointly run J.P. Morgan & Company's worldwide networks. Sprint Corporation does the same for the Anglo-Dutch consumer products manufacturer Unilever Group. MCI Communications Corporation runs computer-maker Sun Microsystem's Pacific Rim network operations. General Electric Company is doing "God's work" in running the global net of the Vatican. Since most companies must hire one networking expert for every twenty-five employees who use a PC on a network, economies can be significant. J.P. Morgan estimates that it will save $12 million in operating costs over five years. Improved data-networking efficiencies can also enhance the ratios of costs to benefits from product development, test marketing, and product standardization on a global basis.

Companies are looking at all their nonstrategic capabilities to determine the smallest number they must keep to support their cores and how many of the remainder they can outsource. Du Pont has outsourced many of its project engineering and design functions to Morrison Knudson; AT&T has outsourced its credit card processing to Total Systems Services; Northern Telecom has outsourced its electronic component manufacturing to Comptronix, which also outsources electronic components for computer manufacturers and makers of communications equipment; Mobil and most of the other major petrochemical processors have outsourced their refinery maintenance work to Serv-Tech, which won the jobs by proving that its crews could minimize downtime from periodic plant maintenance so that its fees would be less than the costs of its clients' own maintenance; and Whirlpool has outsourced its distribution center management to Kenco Group.

Electronic Data Systems (EDS) is operating as an outsourced computer service for Blue Cross & Blue Shield of

Massachusetts, with first-year savings of $25 million in processing health insurance claims. EDS supplies and operates all the systems and equipment needed for claims processing as well as maintaining membership records and responding to customer inquiries. The year-one savings accounted for 7.5 percent of Blue Cross operating costs for the system. This ongoing stream of freed-up money will be used to strengthen Blue Cross finances.

Outsourcing the management of public sector operations, called privatization, is also becoming big business. Private companies are managing state and city facilities instead of simply selling to them, taking assets off government books for state parks, colleges, and prisons. Public services are also being contracted out for construction projects, solid waste collection, janitorial and security services for public buildings, energy and water systems, data processing, health and medical services—just about everything from airports to zoos. Direct cost savings are averaging between 10 and 40 percent, with the most labor intensive services making up the high end.

Concentrating on Core Functions

Among commercial businesses, all kinds of core and noncore activities are being sourced to external service businesses, from engineering to shipping to maintenance and manufacturing. Companies that are shutting down their own manufacturing operations are reallocating their resources to "smart" functions like product development and marketing where they believe they have the best chance to differentiate themselves and earn high margins.

Once free of product manufacturing, companies are turning to their outsourcers to buy materials for them, build products and entire product systems for them, and ship them to customers. Freight forwarders are now packaging the products they ship and even arranging the purchase and assembly of parts that make up the products. This type of complete service package is coming to be expected in the freight forwarding business, forcing forwarders to redefine the nature of their business. Their customers have gone beyond saying to them, "We don't want to ship it ourselves." They are now saying "We don't want to make it either." For the forwarders, what began as a fringe opportunity for higher margins has become an essential requirement for being in the business.

Outsourcing can be extremely specific. Imperial Oil outsources its mainframe computing operations to Electronic Data Systems Corporation but has awarded its desktop computer operations to Digital Equipment Corporation. Outsourcing can also be exceedingly complex. IBM manages Zale Corporation's data operations. It runs Zale's data center, operates the point of sale systems in Zale's 2,000 jewelry stores that enter orders and check credit, and provides Zale with back-up disaster recovery services and industry-specific business consulting services.

In many outsourcing agreements, the facility manager takes over the management of a customer's existing system and, acting as a purchasing agent, acquires new equipment for his client as a systems integrator. In other instances, the outsourcer buys outright the client's operation and hires some of its key employees. Continental Bank, Cummins Engine, Greyhound Lines, Southland Corporation, and General Dynamics have turned all their computing operations and key employees over to facility managers. Cummins outsources in order "to focus our people on making engines and not running computers." Kodak got its computer operations off the books as well as off the premises so that its people could "get on with more strategic operations such as making photographic film and other imaging technologies." As this kind of back-to-the-core thinking flourishes, two or three facility managers can forseeably end up controlling most of the computing power in the United States.

Supplementing Customer Resources

Managers who are receptive to having their facilities and categories managed by outsourcers see it as a competitive advantage. As the major players in each industry grow larger through acquisitions and consolidations within their industries, their increased size causes overwhelming organizational complexities. Even when megacorps decentralize, they end up with a handful of billion-dollar business units instead of a single multibillion-dollar monolith. There are always too many business lines and functions to manage and never enough top-notch managers to go around.

When you act as an outsource manager, you supplement your customers' scarcest resource. This escalates you all the way up the value chain to its highest point, the point where a company's growth is planned and managed. Your management skills become the key capability in reducing unnecessary costs in a client's operations and expanding revenue sources. Because these values are financial, they take you right to the heart of your clients' businesses. This puts you in a far more partnerable position than the operational performance values you would be able to add by manufacturing, selling, and installing products for these same customers.

When you manage a customer's assets or relieve him of the need to own them at all, you perform a similar function to your customer managers—controlling the contribution of an operation to the business as a whole. This gives you a parity with them that no product-based supplier can claim.

The central question for you to answer as a candidate for facility management is, *What assets can I make more competitive in a current customer's operations by managing them for him?* Underutilized and undervalued assets tie up customer cash and tie down management talent. Can you take them off a customer's books? If you can, you can increase his cash flows. Can you give customer line-of-business managers access to broader or richer markets than they can reach? If so, you may be able to convert their operation from a cost center to a profit center as IBM is doing by opening Kodak's data center to other companies that do not want to build or maintain large computing infrastructures of their own. Whatever revenues Kodak receives from data-profitcentering will add to the contribution being made by its minimum annual savings objective of 15 percent from outsourcing.

Proving Enchanced Contribution

When you take on the management of a customer's assets, you relieve yourself of the burden of having to sell your own assets to him. If you make computers like NCR, you will never again have to sell them by the box. Instead, you will be able to sell a data center management plan and move your computers into the billing and collection functions, or forecasting and inventory functions, that it covers. If you make diagnostic equipment for hospitals (like Hewlett-Packard), you will be able to sell an intensive care center management plan or a pain management plan and integrate your equipment into it.

If you make cigarettes, as Philip Morris does, you will be able to sell a tobacco products category management plan to your major supermarket customers and never have to sell a case of your cigarettes to them again. If you make health and beauty aids like Johnson & Johnson, you will be able to sell an HBA category management plan to the same supermarket chains and never have to sell a case of your adhesive bandages to them again.

In each of these plans, you will be trading on your business management capabilities rather than your product manufacturing capabilities. The fact that you are Philip Morris and make Marlboro brand cigarettes or J&J and make Band-Aid brand adhesive bandages will give you prior "proposal rights." But it will take more than Marlboros and Band-Aids to answer the customer's question, *Are you the best manager of this part of my business?* How much do you know about how I make money from it? How good are you at integrating its products? How much more of a profit will you enable it to contribute to my business as a whole?

Your business management plans for client facilities and categories will be used by them as incremental overlays to their strategic business plans. Take out the costs of this function, your plan says. Here are our incremental contributions to your profit, over and above your strategic plan. Add these incremental revenues as our plan says. Here are your expanded contributions to profits over and above your strategic plan. Add the cost savings and revenues together. This is our added value to your strategic growth.

In the role of a facility manager, you will be able to go before your customers with an entirely new set of specifications to sell. Some of them will look like this:

- Systems acquisition costs saved
- Overhead costs saved
- Utilities costs saved
- Manpower costs saved
- Consumables costs saved
- Maintenance costs saved
- Revenues and earnings expanded

In each case, you will have to prove to customers why you are a better buy as a manager than their current internal managers or a competitive facility manager. A cost-benefit analysis such as the model shown in Figure 5-2 is the standard method for proving how much and how soon you can add incremental profits to a customer facility or business category if it comes under your management. This is the same model that also serves systems integrators and process reengineers. The typical analysis shows a customer how much value he can plan on realizing in return for the investment he places in your management plan and how the profits from his increased cash flows will add up annually. Cost-benefit analyses that show these contributions act as "spec sheets" for facility and category managers. They provide major support for a customer's conversion to becoming a client.

The customer's investment will depend on which of three models you propose for the management of his facility:

1. As a client, he continues to own the facility and you contract with him to integrate its systems, reengineer its work flows, and manage it for a fee plus royalties based on performance. You can retain some or all of his people.
2. He sells you the facility outright or makes a low-

interest loan to you and continues to be its customer.
You can also serve other customers.

3. He spins out the facility and makes you an equity-
holding co-owner with him in a freestanding joint
venture that converts his former cost center into an
autonomous profit center. You will be a co-investor
with your client in the new corporate entity as well as
his co-manager.

Under model number 1, you may need to be prepared to
take on added costs in as many as four categories:

1. *Dedicated facilities* in which you set aside a trained
management team plus a work force and an exclusive
plant and office facility that will be immune from
interruption or disruption.
2. *R&D help* to create new customer products or processes that meet your client's competitive objectives.
3. *Customized products* to meet your client's needs.
4. *Inventory management* to provide just-in-time deliveries, with a just-in-case managed reserve.

Proposing Facility Management

A proposal to manage a customer's facility or business category must be presented as a business proposition before the
customer can be converted to a client. As a business case, it
must set financial and operational objectives, define the
critical success factors that will determine realization of the
objectives, and prescribe the single best solution that will
affect the critical factors most cost-effectively. The solution's
technology will come second. Your agenda will look like this:

• *Set objectives.* Calculate revised bottom-line contributions that the managed facility or category will make to
customer competitiveness in terms of:

1. Financial performance contributions to costs and revenues.

2. Operational performance contributions to quality, productivity, and customer satisfaction that will yield the financial contributions.

• *Identify critical success factors.* Define the minimum number of functions you require to be under your management that will account for the maximum amount of improved contribution in the minimum amount of time at minimum investment by outlining:

1. The best place to start to maximize short-term results without compromising long-term success.
2. A step-by-step management plan.

• *Design the single best solution.* Develop the one best solution that is most likely to achieve the objectives of the managed facility or category by acknowledging the solution's critical success factors in three models:

1. A model of the single-source management team that will implement the single best solution and achieve its objectives according to the planned financial and operational models the team will manage.
2. A financial pro-forma model to prototype the economic contributions from facility or category management, showing a before-and-after cost-benefit analysis of the annual cash flows derived from cost reduction or revenue expansion along the lines of Figure 5-2.
3. An operational model to prototype the functional contributions from facility or category management, showing a before-and-after performance analysis of the annual improvements in quality, productivity, and customer satisfaction that will contribute to the financial model.

Ensuring Margins by Improving Contribution

Your ability to contribute to client profits and a client's ability and willingness to contribute to your margins go hand in hand. One is the reciprocal of the other.

The internal costs of operating the processes that you sell into—costs you never see as a product-based supplier—can be margin killers for you. If you sell to hospitals, every dollar they spend with you to buy your products costs them an average of another dollar to move it through their distribution and disposal systems. When hospital customers cannot tolerate these costs any longer, they look to their suppliers to help them by cutting back on product costs. This erodes the margins of their suppliers and still leaves hospital managers with cost-ineffective distribution and disposal systems.

You can become the manager of the part of your customers' supply flow that you affect if you can improve the contribution that the operation makes to the customer's operating statement. At one and the same time, you can ensure your margins.

Your business management proposals will sound like this: What if we can lower your handling and holding costs on our products by $1.5 million a year—will you let us manage their supply for you? The savings will come from reductions you will be able to make in staff, lower inventory, the ability to convert freed-up storerooms to revenue-generating space—in the case of hospitals, to patient care—and cost benefits from improved distribution and disposal procedures. In return, we will be compensated by a management fee of 30 percent of the savings we achieve for you.

The key element in your hospital proposal will be a just-in-time stockless inventory system under which you deliver products on a daily basis direct to the hospital departments and nursing stations on the wards where they are used. You become the inventory manager of your customers' bulk storage warehousing functions for your products. It is only a short step from there to manage stockless inventories for related products that flow through the same distribution process to the same customer departments.

In order to have on hand the management resources to staff a managed customer facility, you will have to set down novel qualifications such as the ones advertised by Honeywell's Commercial Buildings Group for its health care facilities managers:

"Work on-site at the client's health care facility, hospital, or medical center. Be responsible for managing the integration of equipment and work processes into a Total Systems Approach that functions hand-in-hand with the operation of the facility. Administrative and technical responsibilities include management of people and finances as well as overseeing the functioning and maintenance of energy and environmental control systems, electrical and mechanical systems, telecommunications systems, biomedical services, and security. Specific duties will involve reducing operating costs by providing necessary recommendations and technical resource management to hospital departments. This position functions in a consultant capacity."

Acquiring Management Data

Your success as a facility or category manager will be based on what you know about a customer operation that you want to manage and what you know about how to manage it. Facility management is data dependent, relying on two classifications of knowledge:

1. *Knowledge about your customer.* You must know the current contributions to customer profits, both positive and negative, that are being made by the operations you propose to manage when you convert a customer to a client. What are they contributing to total costs? What are they contributing to revenues and earnings? How do these contributions compare to the customer's industry norms and to his major competitors' norms?

2. *Knowledge about your own business.* You must know the contributions your managers can make to a customer's operation you propose to manage. How much cost can they reduce? How much revenue and earnings can they expand? What complementary and competitive products can add the most to your values when they are integrated with them? What is the optimal configuration of business partnerships with other product and service suppliers that will compose

the most cost-effective solutions for your customer operations?

In both categories of knowledge, you will need macrodata and microdata. If you want to manage a manufacturing function or a manufacturing-based business for your client, you will have to begin to fill your macrodatabase with broadscale answers to questions like these:

- How do cycle times affect operations in this type of business:
  — Product design cycles, from conceiving an original product concept to releasing its design to engineering?
  — Product development cycles, from product design to commercial prototype?
  — Manufacturing cycles, from materials assembly to finished goods?
  — Inventory cycles, from stocking to restocking?
  — Order fulfillment cycles, from order receipt to shipped goods?
  — Sales cycles, from initial customer contact to closed sales?
  — Billing and collection cycles, from billing date to collection of accounts receivable?

- How do meantimes affect operations in this type of business:
  — Meantime between start-ups of successive new product development projects?
  — Meantime between product development and manufacturing?
  — Meantime between manufacturing line changeovers?
  — Meantime between downtimes?
  — Meantime between new product releases?

When you get down to microdatabasing, you will have to know the answers to much more finite questions:

- What is the average cost of each downtime? How much money can be saved by extending the meantime between downtimes by each one percent improvement?
- What is the average cost of fulfilling each order? What is the average opportunity cost of each day's delay? How much money can be earned by condensing the meantime between order receipt and fulfillment by each one day of improvement?

If you want to manage a grocery category for supermarket customers, your macrodatabase will have to be able to answer questions like these:

- Which brands are growing and declining in our category and what is causing their growth or decline? What are the roles played by their pricing, promotion, shelf position, and display?
- Where are our customers' major sources of cost in operating the category? Where are they making their major revenues and earnings? What are their sales, stock levels, gross margins, markups, and markdowns? How do our major customers compare with each other in product-by-product sales across the category? What accounts for the differences: pricing, display, space allocation, or stock levels?

The microdata you will need to know will be exceedingly more detailed:

- What are the most profitable category mixes that can build the business best? What are the top sellers? What is the best markdown management schedule for the slow sellers? What is the optimal mix between high turn–low margin and low turn–high margin brands? What is the optimal ratio of stock on hand to purchase levels in order to prevent overstocking or stockouts?
- What are the best shelf allocations? What are the most profitable shelf sets and floor sets? What is the optimal ratio between share of category and share of space?

• What are the best pricing schemes? What is the effect of price elasticity on volume and profits? What are the most profitable prices?

• What is the optimal mix of advertising and promotions? What television, radio, newspaper, direct mail and event combinations build category business most cost-effectively? What are the best combinations of advertising and display; of reduced prices and advertising and display? What are the contributions made by variations in advertisement size, placement, and timing? What products are worth advertising; what extra advertising allowances from vendors are worth negotiating?

• What are the key brands within the category and who are their key vendors? What does each brand contribute to total category sales, direct product profits, and gross margins measured against its percent of total category shelf space? Which vendors contribute the most to category profits by their shipment schedules, discounts and allowances, in-store displays, sales staffing, markups, advertising, defect control, and their strategies for reducing our customers' buying costs?

Trading-Off Values

When a customer outsources a facility or category of his business and becomes a client of its manager, the customer gives up the direct costs of operating his facility and some if not all of the opportunity costs of unrealized revenues. He can also give up opportunity costs from allocating his scarcest resource, his management talent, to noncore operations. Customers trade off giving up control of their operations to gain relief from these costs and inefficiencies.

Not all operations are outsourceable. In spite of competitive advantages, customers may still prefer to retain control of some operations that they deem to be strategic resources, and therefore critical success factors, rather than cede them outside. What constitutes a critical success operation is often a subjective decision. Some customers say that data processing is a critical factor. Others say that only some aspects of data processing are critical. Customers are not always sure of what it means to have operational control. It is sometimes more perceptual than real. In regard to its outsourced information technology systems, Kodak says retrospectively that "we only thought we had control. We used to spend two weeks per year on capital issues, competing for resources. Now we don't buy capital anymore. We can devote those two additional weeks to strategic issues of integrating technology with our businesses and leveraging information systems as a corporate asset."

This same discovery is encouraging customers to relinquish the traditional need to manage all their assets internally and to regard facility and category management as a common make-or-buy decision. One criterion will be final: Who does it best, us or them?

Each company's search for its commercial core will go on relentlessly, providing you with expanding service opportunities. Costs will drive it. So will the pressure to seize a competitive advantage, which means getting all the way into managing what you do best and getting all the way out of everything else. The businesses of the 1990s will end up being composed of the smallest number of operations they must manage for themselves, just as they will be manufacturing for themselves the smallest number of products and staffing the smallest number of people. Mature commodity products that generate cash flows but no growth prospects will be prime candidates for outsourcing. Businesses that are strategically noncritical because they are not based on any proprietary know-how will also be candidates for outsourcers who can make them strategically critical—and therefore profitable—by managing them as core businesses of their own.

6

The Flight of Businesses From Products

The flight of margins from products is acquiring a correlate in the flight of businesses from products. This is more than simply subjugating products to a service. It means that going product-less entirely is becoming a valid strategic option to going margin-less.

Product-free companies are becoming increasingly common. In the computer industry, MIPS is an example of a computerless computer company. A multimillion-dollar publicly traded corporation, MIPS has no in-house manufacturing capability of its own. It designs microchips and licenses their production and sales to other businesses in return for royalty fees.

Another high-technology company, Rambus, Inc., is licensing its technology to manufacturers of memory chips rather than manufacture them itself. Rambus plans to make money from licensing fees and royalties instead of chip sales because "the world doesn't need another supplier of memory chips."

Product-less companies start without the financial burdens imposed by manufacturing. Up to three-quarters of a product's cost may be taken up by making it. Development costs have to be added on top. The more innovative a business is, and the more vigorously it presses on to Six Sigma quality, the higher its development costs will be. After corporate overhead is factored in, little may be left of gross margins.

Traditional thinkers about business consider product-less companies to be "hollowed out" because their cores are vacant of manufacturing processes. Without manufacturing, they believe a business can have no heart. But should manufacturing, or any other capability, ever be positioned as a company's core? Should it not be a peripheral asset, supportive of the true core that is represented by the competitive values that a business adds to its customers? If your managers are busy creating value for their customers and building their entire businesses around it, the question to ask about manufacturing is: What does it contribute to the value-adding process? Unless the answers are compelling, a business risks becoming stuffed with manufacturing costs that its hollowed-out margins will never be able to repay.

The issue may well come down to the decision of where you are willing to accept hollowness: in your physical plant or in your earnings per sale.

Some companies are freeing themselves from products another way: They sell products under their own name that they do not manufacture. As outsourcing of customer facilities grows in popularity as a service business, more companies in every industry will seek to divest themselves of the costs of manufacturing and become unalloyed service providers.

As a result, two distinct tiers of businesses are coming into being. The first tier sells a service that includes products that the second tier makes. Tier number one is composed of systems integrators, process reengineers, and facility or category managers. Tier two companies are staying in manufacturing. The trade-off they are making is to adopt rigid cost controls and switch to scrapless, laborless highly automated flexible manufacturing systems that are unburdened by sales and marketing costs. This is the only way they will still be able to find margins, however slim, in their boxes.

In a reversal of the Peter Principle, each tier will be working at its highest level of competence. Tier one companies will be very good at providing a growth service. Tier two companies will be very good at developing, manufacturing, and delivering the high-quality products that tier one will apply, install, and implement as component parts of integrated systems, reengineered processes, and managed facilities.

Tier two companies will find it advantageous to start small or get as small as possible and stay smaller than their total opportunity so that they can build out or squeeze out all excess costs. This will ensure greater productivity based on the ability to create more earnings with fewer workers. Each worker will be able to earn more as well as contribute more to the business. Rightsizing right from the start will turn out to be the secret of tier two profitability.

Tier two companies will have to adopt a new three-phase life cycle plan for each major product in order to give it every chance to maintain acceptable margins throughout the cycle.

At conception, a product's midlife terminal date will have to be set to mark its maximum margin opportunity. The terminal date predicts the most likely onset of the product's maturity. Under this self-imposed time pressure, a product's managers will have to work backwards from introduction to plan a three-track course to its eventual replacement:

1. A Kaizen continuous-improvement strategy to achieve a minimum 10 percent reduction in product cost by the sixth month after introduction and a minimum 10 percent improvement in reliable performance by month twelve. This will help ensure the short-term sustainability of a product's original margins.
2. A yeastbud strategy to logically extend the original product into a family of related products and product-related systems. This will further help ensure margin continuity.
3. A second-stage new product development strategy to be implemented before the predicted onset of maturity. This will help ensure a regeneration of margins.

In this way, lucky tier two companies may be able to extract the equivalent of three product evolutions from a single product, each at survivable margins.

This three-for-one approach requires a vigilant hands-on grasp of each product, yeastbudding it at exactly the right time to take advantage of maximum demand buildup and innovating it just before maturity sets in, even a day sooner rather than a day later.

American product-based companies are, on the whole, ill prepared or reluctant to practice three-phase life-cycle planning. They are finding that they have their hands full with the Kaizen phase. Japanese companies have had almost half a century of experience making money being product-based. Although the industrial policy covenants of their Ministry of International Trade & Industry have made many aspects of strategic management superfluous for them, they have become experts in serially rebirthing high-quality manufactured products before their margins wear thin. By now they may have acquired all the necessary attributes to be the preeminent tier two companies in the world.

Looking at the global business community in this way may open the eyes of American managers. It may also open opportunities for them in the new options of the 1990s.

If you act fast, you can apply to be a tier one leader by transforming your product-based business into a service. This will make your margins dependent on improving profits for your customers. Your other option is to choose tier two or fall into it by default. This will make your margins dependent on improving your own cost controls, your own quality, your own productivity, and the efficiency of every person, product, and process in your organization. Your margin for error will be as slim as your margins from sales.

Will you consult or be consulted to? Will you integrate customer systems or be integrated into them? Will you reengineer customer processes or be reengineered out of them? Will you manage customer facilities and categories of business or will you be managed from tier one? If push comes to shove, which will you choose: to go product-less into the future or to go profit-less?

Index

[Page numbers in italics refer to figures.]